Ethical Leadership:
A Competitive Edge

Richard Bellingham Ed.D.
Barry Cohen, Ph.D.

Published by   Human Resource Development Press, Inc.
                22 Amherst Road
                Amherst, Massachusetts 01002

ISBN No. 0-87425-144-3

First Printing, October, 1990

Cover Design by Cora Drew, Old Mill Graphics
Production Services by Susan Kotzin

DEDICATION

This book is dedicated to our parents:

Earl Bellingham
Dorothy Bellingham
Dorothy Cohen
Sam Cohen

ACKNOWLEDGMENTS

In preparing this book, we owe a special debt of gratitude to:

— our families who love us and inspire us to love.

— Robert Carkhuff, Ph.D., an ethical exemplar.

— David Olive, our editor, who provided excellent editorial feedback and valuable ideas to incorporate.

— our reviewers: Mark Edwards, Len Brooks, Jack McConnell, Dave Villepique, Cal Jackson and Helen Leighton who provided invaluable contributions during various stages of the book.

— several people at Northern Telecom: Margaret Kerr, Tim Williams, Art Fitzgerald and Dave Tostenson who provided support, encouragement, and suggestions along the way.

TABLE OF CONTENTS

FORWARD
A QUESTION OF ETHICS

The question of ethics is the question of the twentieth century.

In a country as diverse as the United States, finding the ethical stance is no simple task. Choices and dilemmas crowd the ethical arena: the rights of the spotted owl versus the jobs of thousands in the lumber industry; the rights of the woman versus the rights of the unborn; industry as a provider of jobs and services to its communities versus its responsibilities to return profits to shareholders. The list could continue indefinitely and at some point has an impact on all of us.

Indeed, the question of ethics is no longer an academic word exchange, restricted to university settings, but plays out daily in the "real world" as events such as Watergate, Iran Contra, and the Mike Milliken junk bond legacy continue to remind us.

Twisting our way around ethical conflicts is now an art form. We acknowledge, rather arrogantly sometimes, that the answer is a business one, or a political one, military one, or even a religious one. We decouple the ethical question from the discussion. We stop asking "what is right?" or "what is legal?" or "what can we get away with?".

In traditional and homogenous societies, ethical standards are embodied deeply in the culture. Concepts of right and wrong are clearly delineated. In America, the ethical standard is a moving target. As a response, we often let the situation define the response.

It is a long road from the view that business exists for the purpose of creating value for shareholders to the view that companies with a strong ethical stance have the competitive edge. Indeed, making ethical practices a corporate value enriches the corporate soul and the bottom line. But Drs. Cohen and Bellingham have us believing just that. However, instead of merely *describing* the ethical companies a là *In Search of Excellence,* Cohen and Bellingham *prescribe* how to become one.

They are firm believers that strong leadership coupled with articulated values and vision can transform an organization from moribund to exemplar. This book is too important to take lightly or to dismiss as another post Milliken-Boesky tome.

Workforce 2000 is almost upon us. The United States of America is struggling toward reality, and the cold war has thawed. American business and industry will face challenges unparalled in our history. Clear vision and strong ethical principles will have to be the twin anchors to usher in the New Age. This book is the blueprint.

Anderson Kurtz
Cambridge, Massachusetts
1990

PREFACE
MAKING THE RIGHT CHOICES

This book positions ethics as a competitive edge; and it challenges the assumption that ethics and profitability are unrelated. The book also challenges the reader to respond to new ethical issues as moral and business opportunities. By so doing, leaders will develop an organizational culture that thrives because it is ethical.

Increasingly, contemporary organizations realize that ethics and profits are not conflicting concerns. As awareness grows about the relationship between ethical leadership and competitive advantage, corporations are emphasizing one or another aspect of ethics (e.g., environment). Yet, real competitive edge requires a comprehensive ethical leadership: people, customers, and communities. Top executives note that good ethics is a prime corporate asset. They understand that a solid ethical foundation is one of the important components for long-term corporate success.[1]

We will define ethics as:

- the discipline of dealing with what is good and bad, and with moral duty and obligation.
- the principles of conduct governing an individual or a group.[2]

At its core, ethics involves the discipline of decency. And the essence of ethics is independent thinking and questioning.[3]

Business ethics is deeply concerned with both moral values and moral actions. Moral values are basic ideals that are considered desirable or worthwhile for human interaction. Moral actions are the overt expressions and applications of these underlying values. Therefore, the notion that, as businesspersons, we should not deceive or mislead our customers is a moral value. Behaving honestly and fairly toward our customers is a moral action. Business ethics is called into question when the moral values or the accompanying moral actions of organizational decision-makers conflict with the commonly accepted standards of society.[4]

The fundamental issues related to ethical leadership can be categorized in this 2 x 2 grid:

Ethics

	Good	Bad
Good		
Bad		

Business

Decisions that fall into the Good/Good or the Bad/Bad cell tend to be easy to make. After all, why wouldn't leaders support decisions that make good business sense and are highly ethical. And for all those decisions that are highly unethical and make for bad business, voting "no" would also be a simple matter. When leaders fail to make the right choices, for instance, paying employees fairly (good/good) or dumping garbage on main street (bad/bad), the poor choice can be attributed politely to unenlightened thinking or—not so politely—to stupidity.

On the other hand, those issues that fall into the Good/Bad or the Bad/Good cells present an entirely different challenge. This grey area is where many executives wallow in ethical ambiguity.

The introduction of the Valdez Principles in September, 1989, by the Coalition for Environmentally Responsible Economies (CERES) implores the public to raise its sights to higher ethical goals. The Valdez Principles rose from the aftermath of the Exxon Valdez oil spill disaster off the coast of Alaska. The concept is to develop standards of responsible behavior on which a broad range of companies can be compared. This concept has a precedent with the Sullivan Principles, a voluntary set of guidelines adopted by the largest companies in the U.S., governing conduct by American businesses in South Africa. The guidelines were introduced in 1977 by the Rev. Leon Sullivan, a Philadelphia minister and a member of the board of General Motors Corporation. That model had been introduced with the support of several large global companies as a progressive response to the position of protesters who wanted the companies to cut all ties with South Africa.

The Valdez Principles, however, are far more sweeping in their scope and objectives, as well as being more vague in their language.[5] The principles provide excellent targets for change, but they don't impose absolute commitments. Companies can subscribe to the intent without locking themselves into action. Thus, the principles could become a public placebo.

VALDEZ PRINCIPLES

Protection of the Biosphere: Signatories will try to eliminate pollutants that damage the air, water or earth.

Sustainable Use of Natural Resources: Pledges use of renewable resources, conservation of non-renewable materials and preservation of biological diversity.

Reduction and Disposal of Waste: Pledges minimizing and safely disposing of hazardous wastes.

Wise Use of Energy: Calls for energy efficient products and processes.

Risk Reduction: Pledges reducing environmental risks and preparing for accidents.

Marketing of Safe Products and Services: Pledges disclosure of environmental impact of products and services.

Damage Compensation: Pledges restoration of damaged environments and compensation for human injury.

Disclosure: Pledges disclosure of accidents and hazards and protection against reprisal for employees who report them.

Environmental Directors and Managers: Companies agree that at least one board member will be an environmental expert. A senior executive for environmental affairs will also be named.

Assessment and Annual Audit: Pledges annual environmental audit of worldwide operation. Audit is to be made public.

Some businesses are operating on very thin profit margins. They may decide that, while they support the concept of the Valdez Principles, they just can't afford to commit to them. Although such a decision may backfire in the long run, some businesses may experience such tremendous, short-term earnings pressures that it will be difficult for them to abide by the principles. Others may feel that the principles expose them to excessive risks. And some just won't care. In some companies, a commitment to the Valdez principles may take them from a profit position to a loss position in the short term. Clearly, these commitments pose hard choices for management.

Ethical leaders will want to explore their motives and values in relation to issues such as the Valdez Principles. They will be interested in "right attitudes" and "right thinking." They will be less inclined to make behavioral shifts because it is manipulative and market sensitive. They will make ethical choices because it is the right thing to do and it happens to make good business sense.

There's more than enlightened self-interest at work among leaders who conform to rigorous, ethical guidelines and pressures. What really motivates them is an interest in developing ethical attitudes toward living and working. While it appears that the market will respond favorably to apparent changes in ethical behaviors, the ethical leader is more concerned that ethical values dominate management thinking. The ethical leader understands that a true change in business ethics will require a frontal assault on who we are, not just token efforts to increase knowledge about what one can and cannot do according to a code of ethics.

Moreover, codes of ethics in many corporations have had little impact on employee actions, largely because these codes have sought only to protect firms from the actions of their employees and have stressed "legalese"; most codes have neglected the important ethical issues related to culture, environment, people, customers and communities.[6]

Two critical principles emerge from this discussion: 1) ethical initiatives that come entirely from a "business" perspective may have temporary effects, but will erode when business pressures or market data demand a change in strategy. 2) If ethical initiatives originate for ethical reasons, then changes will be more lasting and will be less influenced by market manipulations.

This book will demonstrate that:

- more opportunities exist in the Good/Good cell than we realize.

- few companies succeed long term that operate in the Good business/Bad ethics mode.

- more understanding is needed for the hard choices that exist in the Good ethics/Bad business mode.

For example, what decision should a major employer make, upon whom a small town is economically dependent, when that firm discovers it is a major polluter in the area. If it closes down, the residents of the town may experience severe economic hardship, their quality of life may deteriorate, and self-esteem be diminished. If the company's plant remains open, however, the environment will continue to be violated.

While this book focuses on the hard choices of leaders, managers at all organizational levels are affected by ethical issues. However, one major study concludes that executives and middle managers differ significantly in their ethical views.[7]

1. Middle managers are more likely than executives to believe that their behavior should be based on what is right and just for any other person in a similar situation.

2. Executives are more likely than middle managers to believe in bluffing and taking advantage of all legal opportunities and widespread practices or customs.

3. Executives are more likely than middle managers to believe in their "gut feelings" in a given situation.

4. Executives are less likely than middle managers to believe one should take selfish actions or be motivated by personal gains in business dealings.

5. Executives are more likely than middle managers to believe that some overall profit-based goal must justify a moral transgression, i.e., a "wrong" choice must generate significant earnings to make it worthwhile.

6. Middle managers are more likely than executives to believe in seizing advantage of an opportunity without respect to social convention and laws.

A majority of the managers in two separate studies have reported feeling pressures from the demands of their jobs to compromise their personal ethical standards.[8,9] Other investigators found that ethical considerations were less important aspects of management jobs than traditional management functions and skills such as decision making, initiative and problem solving. However, ethics were rated as more important than activities such as written communications, awareness of external affairs, concern for quality, customer satisfaction and group interaction skills. Managers clearly viewed ethical analysis, decision-making and action as important and regular parts of their work lives.[10]

This book will encourage leaders and managers, who seek to be leaders, to consider the personal principles on which they base their decisions. It will help them to assess the level of ethical functioning in their organizations and explore how they can gain competitive advantage by developing an "ethical edge". The following scale will not only help leaders determine, in a general way, their current level of ethical functioning, but will also prompt them to decide what their goal is in relation to ethics.

A RANGE OF ETHICAL GOALS
FOR ORGANIZATIONS

5.0   Become an Ethical Exemplar
4.0   Create an Ethical Culture
3.0   Provide Proactive Ethics Programs
2.0   Comply with the Law
1.0   Stay Out of Trouble

The premise of this book is that a level four or level five goal is required to turn an ethical burden into a competitive edge.

The book has five chapters: Creating an Ethical Culture, Winning Through People, Winning With Customers, Winning for Communities, and Action Steps. General rating scales for each of these areas are included in the overview section of each chapter. Rating scales for each aspect of these general topics are included in Appendix A. Examples of codes of ethics are contained in Appendix B.

Chapter One addresses the relationship of ethics to corporate culture. It shows how vision, values and norms are the critical ingredients in any approach to organizational change related to ethics.

Chapter Two addresses company-employee relationships. This section covers the principles of developing people, promoting health and safety, creating a sense of balance, and valuing differences.

Chapter Three addresses ethical considerations of customer relationships. It addresses principles related to product development, manufacturing and marketing.

Chapter Four discusses ways in which organizations deal with the communities in which they are located. This section covers enhancing the environment, contributing to community resources and participating in community organizations.

Chapter Five provides action steps for the ethical executive. It suggests strategies for transforming principles into action.

Each chapter is divided into five parts: an Introduction, an Overview, the Issues, the Exemplars and a Challenge. These five parts give the reader a general idea of how each of these areas can contribute to competitive advantage, provide a rationale for taking action in these areas, and demonstrate what other companies have done to enhance their profitability through exemplary ethics.

Organizations need to take a hard look at the way they do business, and decide what changes are required. They need to understand explicitly the issues related to ethical behavior now and in the future. Leaders need to have a vision of how ethics can create new possibilities for the future growth of the business, and they need to understand what steps they can take to lay the groundwork for connecting ethics and traditional strategy in every phase of the business.

The book also contains several ideas that the authors believe would represent not only a new ethical statement, but would also be very profitable. We hope that decision-makers assess their companies' current ethical status on the scales provided. The authors believe that leaders who develop ethically focused companies will be the ones rewarded by exciting new business horizons.

INTRODUCTION
DOING WELL BY DOING GOOD

In 1988, the Conference Board completed a study of corporate ethics based on an international survey and interviews with 300 leading companies. The report revealed how these companies define ethical issues, respond to ethical dilemmas, develop and communicate codes of ethics and design ethics training programs. The median 1985 sales figure for these companies was $1.26 billion. Two thirds of those responding to the questionnaire were CEOs; the other third were senior-level executives. One result of the survey was to reveal what executives considered to be ethical issues for business and to rank the importance of those issues in the next five years. As you can see in Table 1, the emphasis on ethics and the business world has been on doing the right thing simply *because* it's the right thing. This book expands that concept, and proposes that doing the right thing will provide companies with a competitive edge.

At the top of the "issues" list, with more than 90 percent agreeing that the subject raised ethical questions for business, are employee conflicts of interest, inappropriate gifts to corporate personnel, and sexual harassment. These issues are all addressed in the sample code of ethics contained in Appendix B.

Environmental issues, product and workplace safety, employee health screening, security of company records, and shareholders' interests were cited by more than two thirds of these participants as critical or serious concerns for business in the next five

Table 1

	Percent agreeing this is an ethical issue	Percent who think issue will be critical or serious
Employee conflicts of interest	91	44
Inappropriate gifts to corporate personnel	91	36
Sexual harassment	91	64
Unauthorized payments	85	47
Affirmative action	84	66
Employee privacy	84	50
Environmental issues	82	86
Employee health screening	79	77
Conflicts between company's ethics and foreign business practices	77	46
Security of company records	76	73
Workplace safety	76	70
Advertising content	74	37
Product safety standards	74	78
Corporate contributions	68	31
Shareholder interests	68	70
Corporate due process	65	51
Whistleblowing	63	29
Employment at will	62	59
Disinvestment	59	64
Government contract issues	59	49
Financial and cash management procedures	55	56
Plant/facility closures and downsizing	55	64
Political action committees	55	43
Social issues raised by religious organizations	47	21
Comparable worth (pay equity)	43	41
Product pricing	42	44
Executive salaries	37	32

years. All of these issues will be addressed in Chapters One through Four of this book. The most disturbing aspect of Table 1 is the large percentage of respondents who did not consider certain items as ethical issues, e.g., 26 percent think product safety is not an ethical issue.

Some organizations have taken a defensive posture in relation to these ethical issues. They see new developments in ethical awareness as a threat to the status quo. Many others, however, are taking a proactive stance to ensure they are doing the right things, and to benefit from improvements in employee and customer relations. Ethical standards have changed rapidly over the past few years and the rate of change is increasing. A review of what has happened on Wall Street and in the American government over the past few years gives a sense of how dramatic those changes are.

Essayist Myron Magnet observed that "as if trapped by a thermal inversion, the ethical atmosphere of business is growing acrid and the inhalation of those pernicious vapors could only lead to ever worse behavior".[1] If that observation has any truth to it, then how can the process be turned around?

John Shad, a former vice-chairman of E.F. Hutton and past chairman of the Securities and Exchange Commission, pledged $30 million to the Harvard Business School to try to find the answer. His gift was for the promotion of the study of business ethics. From his close association with the finance community, Shad publicly declared his disgust with market malfeasances. Shad had strong feelings about how business ought to be done. And one of the things he got for his remarkable contribution was a public forum in which to air his conviction that "ethics pays", and "the marketplace does reward integrity."[2]

It appears that Shad's premise has validity. The results of an analysis of 15 *Fortune* 500 companies in existence at least thirty years that had

1) maintained a written set of principles specifying the company's public service policy, and

2) maintained adherence to those principles for at least a generation,

had an average growth in profits over the 30-year period ending in 1982 of 11 percent. In a roughly comparable period, the balance of *Fortune* 500 companies experienced a growth rate in profits of 6.1 percent.[3]

That study indicated that ethical leadership very likely does provide a competitive edge in business. This book explains why, and enables organizations to determine how they can win the right way.

The media and the public have paid increasing attention to ethics in business over the past several years. And there has been an escalating trend in business to re-examine its corporate consciences. This trend will continue in the 1990s, and the 21st century will usher in a whole new set of expectations that society places on the business community.

Three major developments have acted as catalysts to increase corporate sensitivity to ethical issues: a labor pool that is decreasing in quantity and quality, increasing public attention on ethics, and globalization.

First, as the quantity and quality of the labor pool continues to decline, talented applicants will seek out employers whom they view as acting ethically. As societal values change, job seekers are becoming more and more attuned to the ethics of potential employers. The ethical image of the firm plays a big role in employee selection decisions. In many ways the tables have turned. Applicants are now "selecting" employers instead of vice versa. Thus, 21st century organizations will need to address these changing values, trends and expectations if they are going to be successful in attracting the best people. On a more discouraging note, M.I.T. recently cancelled an elective course on social responsibility because of lack of attendance. Apparently, student passion for ethics has not counter-balanced the need to meet requirements.

Second, consumers are increasingly making buying decisions based on their perception of the seller's corporate conscience. They want to be assured that businesses are good corporate citizens. For example, the Council on Economic Priorities, based in New York, has published a book entitled *Rating America's Corporate Conscience*, which evaluates the companies behind the products that consumers purchase every day.[4] The book enables consumers to select products based on the perceived social responsibility of producers. The Council provides rating scales on the social performance of hundreds of companies based on six criteria.

1. Charitable contributions.

2. Representation of women and minorities on boards of directors and among top corporate officers.

3. Disclosure of social information.

4. Involvement in South Africa.

5. Conventional weapons-related contracting.

6. Nuclear weapons-related contracting.

Brand-name product charts give a simple high/middle/low rating for the manufacturer's relative record on these issues. The product charts are not intended to express any opinion or ratings about the products themselves, but indicate only the Council's "social rating" of the companies that make those products. The book also contains ethics information for investors. A quick guide is provided to some socially responsible funds and investment advisors. This information is intended to influence investors to make social responsibility a key factor in choosing which stocks, bonds and mutual funds should be purchased for their portfolios.

Consumer groups may be forcing ethical issues sooner than anticipated. Books such as *The 100 Best Companies to Work for in America*[5], *Rating America's Corporate Conscience*[6], *The 100 Best Companies to Work for in Canada*[7] and others are starting to influence employment and buying decisions. For example, there are more than a dozen mutual funds in North America which specialize in ethical investing and they enjoyed, in total, a 50 percent surge in capital invested in 1987.[8] These investment funds have a well defined set of criteria to evaluate companies on ethical behavior and social responsibility.[9] Clearly, consumers are becoming more aware of the ethical sensitivity of the companies in which they invest, from whom they purchase and for whom they work. This trend has not reached tidal wave proportions. One company that advises municipalities on the management of their pensions found that when they offered "ethically-invested" funds, very few people bought them. Thus, the pockets of enthusiasm and support have to be broadened.

It does appear that environmental concerns are of paramount importance to investors. The Calvert Social Investment Fund, based in Washington D.C., conducted a survey in 1988 of its 30,000 clients, and found the environment to be their greatest concern by far. The fund, which manages $350 million in assets has applied numerous environmental tests to screen its investments since its founding in 1982. These include a ban on investments in manufacturers of plastic packaging and in companies that are judged to contribute to the destruction of rain forests abroad or old-growth forests in the United States.

And many companies are getting the message. In Canada, 85 percent of the country's largest corporations are making ethical performance disclosures related to products, human resources, environment, community involvement and other factors.[10] This heightened focus on ethics not only reflects an increasing trend toward altruistic motives, but also indicates the possibilities for ethics in economic advantage.

Finally, participating in global markets will require that host countries are satisfied that foreign investors are sensitive to their concerns. Increasingly, North American-based multinationals are finding that countries elsewhere in the world will insist that businesses are responsible in the ways in which they interact with people, communities, stakeholders and customers. Ethical sensitivities are not, after all, restricted to North America. Countries around the world are more and more concerned about their environment, the health and safety of their people, and the ways in which business is conducted. They are demanding appropriate behavior from multinationals.

To bolster this movement, the public in North America, not just the governments of foreign countries, are disturbed by the implications of looming environmental problems abroad, such as the depletion of the ozone layer and the destruction of the Brazilian rain forest. And these North American consumers are focusing their impatience for progress on the North American companies perceived to be implicated in environmental problems occurring offshore. Also, North American governments, in turn, are applying similarly tough standards on foreign-based companies doing business here, e.g. Japanese forest-products companies operating in Alberta, Canada.

These changes have profound implications for the modern corporation. They represent tremendous potential for those companies who act now to seize the advantage. Some companies, of course, already have. James E. Burke, retired chairman of Johnson and Johnson Inc. of New Jersey, states that "there's an important correlation between a corporation's public responsibility and its ultimate financial performance. Although public service is implied in the charter of all American companies, public responsibility, in reality, is a company's very reason for existing." This book contains examples of ethics exemplars in every topic area covered.

Using the principles of ethical leadership as a vehicle for competitive advantage, however, represents an overlooked opportunity for most firms. This opportunity could be one of the significant sources of gain for innovative companies in the next century. And more attention to ethics would go a long way toward increasing productivity.

Leaders have been dealing with ethical issues since their inception. Several factors have influenced how the scope and nature of these issues have changed. The ownership of businesses has changed from single owner/operators living in the host community to a heterogeneous group of stakeholders living all over the world, who may know very little about the company or the communities in which the business operates. Second, the philosophy of running a business has changed from a small-town, homespun notion that "the business operates in the interest of society," to a legalistic, compliance mentality that "action must be legally and morally acceptable." Third, locations of businesses have changed from local manufacturing plants to international service and manufacturing networks. Finally, control of the way businesses are run has changed. Influence has shifted from personal values to heavy governmental regulation. Union and professional codes of ethics exert a powerful influence.[11] In short, there has been an insidious breakdown of connectedness between businesses and the communities in which they reside.

As the year 2000 approaches, we will see an even more rapid evolution of corporate ethics. Corporate ownership will be by international stakeholders. Not only will corporate constitutents represent every area of the world, but they will also be concerned about how the policies and actions of a particular company may affect their part of the planet. Corporate philosophy will become, "you have to do good to do well." There will be a realization that employment and purchasing decisions will be largely influenced by the perceived ethics of the company. Companies will be located all over the world as global markets expand. Goods and services will be produced and provided wherever it makes the most sense to do so.

Finally, the driving values for doing business will be international cooperation and interdependence. Universal connectedness will become more of a reality, and people will realize that actions cannot be seen in isolation. Table 2 summarizes how these factors have changed over time, and projects what businesses can expect by the year 2000.

While ethics awareness is growing, most of the discussion revolves around avoidance issues: loss of consumer confidence, potential for fines, pressure from special interest groups, legal and financial vulnerability of corporate executives and professionals, increasing attention to pollution and negative publicity. Thus, corporations are saying they want to stay out of

Table 2
Evolution of American Business

	Ownership	Ethic	Location	Control
PHASE I **Before** **1800**	single owner living in community	business operates in the interest of society	local	individual values
PHASE II **1800-1900**	close-knit shareholders lliving near community	business is interested in society	regional	community values
PHASE III **1900-1950**	homogeneous shareholders living in the same country	what's good for business is good for country	national	some governmental & union values
PHASE IV **1950-2000**	heterogeneous stakeholders living through-out the world	action must be morally and legally acceptable	multi-national	professional & corporate codes of ethics
PHASE V **2000 +**	international stakeholders	you have to do good to do well	global	international cooperation & interde-pendence

trouble and be in compliance with the law so that they don't lose consumer confidence, get fined, come under pressure from special interest groups, get thrown in jail, be seen as a polluter, or suffer negative exposure in the media.

There tends to be minimal discussion on proactive issues. For example, how can we increase our competitive advantage through an ethical approach? The emphasis is on constraints and obligations rather than opportunities and possibilities. This book addresses the latter.

It should be noted that the current social environment does not support a more proactive approach. There is a corporate paranoia stemming from litigious exploitation of system imperfections. Thus, an inordinate amount of corporate energy is directed toward the avoidance of problems rather than the creation of systemic solutions.

CHAPTER ONE

CREATING AN ETHICAL CULTURE

Introduction

An ethical corporate culture is one in which the vision of the organization includes its employees, its customers and the community. The organization's values and norms support actions consistent with an ethical vision. The ethical perspective is so embedded in how the organization does business that no major business decision is made without consideration of its impact on the employees, the customers and the community. Before exploring how to create such a culture, some discussion of concepts and classifications might be helpful.

Organizational culture is the unseen, unwritten, and unobservable force that is always behind organizational activities, rules and behavior that can be seen and observed.

Culture can be defined as the collection of values and norms that differentiate one group from another. Values constitute the stated principles on which the organization functions. Norms are the accepted, traditional and reinforced standards or behaviors in a given culture. If we accept the definition of ethics as the principles of conduct governing an individual or a group, we can see that the ethical culture in an organization is the collection of principles regarding right and wrong in certain groups. Articulating values and transforming them into norms is the goal of all culture-change efforts.

If an organizational culture is in conflict with ethical guidelines articulated by management, it is easy to see how the existing culture will win, and the initiative for change will falter. The unwritten rules and norms of an organization are far more powerful than concepts and ideas. Thus, if an organization is committed to an ethical approach, it must understand culture and how to change it.

Two American pioneers in this field, Hay and Gray, have done a review of various approaches to business ethics. They contend that ethical orientation can be categorized into three styles: profit maximization, trusteeship and quality of life.[1]

In the "profit maximization" style, management operates out of raw self-interest and is only constrained by legal limits. Money and wealth are the driving values, and people are seen as commodities to be bought and sold. On our scale, this orientation would be classified as staying out of trouble or complying with the law. In this orientation, the organization only focuses on employees, the customer and community when mandated. The primary conditions which permit this view of ethics to result in profits are an economy of scarcity and an abundance of labor. With these conditions, the main goal is to produce a sufficient quantity of products to meet an existing demand. Quality is not the most important issue because, in an economy of scarcity, there is little or no competition for products or services.

In the "trusteeship" style, management sees itself as responsible for achieving an equitable balance among customers, suppliers, creditors, stockholders and the community. Money and people are the driving values and managers recognize that employees have more than just economic needs. On our scale, this orientation to ethics would be classified as providing proactive programs. The primary conditions which permit this view of ethics to result in profits are the use of skilled labor and the participation in strong markets. With this ethical approach the main goal is to maximize technology. Quality is critical because competition is severe. The major pitfall with this view of ethics is the assumption that skilled people who meet or exceed the skill requirements of the business can always be recruited and retained. While this approach considers the ethical implications of actions, it falls far short of creating an ethical culture. Organizations using this approach are always treating employees, customers and the community as a means rather than an interdependent part of the success equation. When the short-term profit motive clashes with the long-term interest of employees, customers and the community, the organization usually chooses the direction that results in the profit—often at a significant cost to itself in the long term.

In the "quality of life" style, leadership assumes a responsibility for its ethics and its values. Enlightened self-interest, employee development, customer productivity and community well-being become the prepotent factors in making decisions; and leaders believe that what is good for society is good for their company. Employee dignity is a predominant concern and people are seen to be as important as money. On our scale, this view of ethics would be classified as creating an ethical culture, and would probably result in the organization becoming an ethical exemplar. The primary conditions which permit this view of ethics to result in profits are empowered people, interdepenence and trust. With these conditions, the main goals are to maximize human and information capital, and use financial capital as a catalyst for future growth. As long as we operate in a free society in which truth is valued and trust achieved, then this style will not only result in the greatest public good, but will also generate the greatest amount of wealth to buy our goods and services and perpetuate the cycle. Leaders who create this type of culture will strengthen the connection between ethics and profits.

In conclusion, taking a cultural approach to ethics means creating the vision, values and norms that support the connection between profits and ethics. This chapter will explore these three ingredients of culture and a process for change.

Overview

Vision

Creating an ethical culture means empowering people to do the right thing for the company, the customer and the community.

These are the assumptions related to the connection between profits and an ethical culture. In an ethical culture, the environment:

- supports the development of human and information capital;

- ensures that all relationships are conducted honestly;

- creates a sense of pride, purpose, and persistence in the organization's goals;

- increases customers' trust, confidence and comfort in doing business with the organization;

- reduces the need for security measures that react to fraud, theft and illegal practices within the organization.

Principles

1. Creating an ethical culture must begin with a vision that includes employees, customers and communities.

2. An ethical culture must be guided by values that anchor the vision.

3. An ethical culture must be supported by norms and policies that influence desired behaviors in the organizational environment.

Rating scale for culture

5.0	Congruence
4.0	Transference
3.0	Behavior Change
2.0	Motivation
1.0	Awareness

Specific scales for rating vision, values and environment are included in Appendix A.

Vision

The Issues

Creating an ethical culture must begin with a vision which boils down to how we view the organization and its relationship to the world. It represents how inclusive we are.

A meaningful and believable vision can go a long way toward mobilizing employee enthusiasm or deflating it. If employees believe their organization has a real sense of purpose, employee pride and perspective will improve. But if employees believe the company is only motivated by profit, their commitment, loyalty and trust will be diminished. After all, if the company "screws" its cutomers, why would employees believe that it wouldn't "screw" them as well?

Over the past twenty years there have been two major forces with significant relevance to ethics. The first force has been an emphasis on short term profits and quarterly results which tends to *limit* an organization's ethical vision. The second force has been a growing sophistication of customers and new demands for customer satisfaction. This focus on the customer tends to promote an expanded vision that includes customers.

Indications of a narrow vision are rampant. Since boards of directors have been under enormous pressure to satisfy shareholders on a quarterly basis, many investments that may have had great potential for long-term return have been abandoned, postponed or set aside. Unfortunately, a good share of those programs would be considered of an ethical nature. As a result, many companies have become more reactionary in their "operating" vision.

This lack of vision has manifested itself in several disturbing internal problems. Corporate cultures driven without regard for people may cause a great deal of individual stress and loss of productivity. The stress that is generated by negative norms and inappropriate management behaviors affects people in three distinct ways.[2] First, there may be a direct effect, manifested in physical problems such as hypertension, ulcers, and cardiovascular disease. Then there is a secondary effect that shows up in certain observable behaviors such as smoking, overeating, drinking too much, or having accidents. Third, this stress may cause people to overreact to physical symptoms and thus engage in illness behavior such as staying home from work, avoiding healthy activity, or being nonproductive. It is important to realize that modifiable risk factors that contribute to positive health behaviors and organizational health include the norms, values, and practices of the workplace and of management, as well as such personal factors as lack of knowledge, skills and motivation. For example, consider the impact:

- *on a person's productivity* when an organization is rigid and autocratic, when it is unclear where a person fits into an organization; or when roles and responsibilities are ambiguous.

- *on organizational productivity* when management does not make use of employees' talents and resources. Conversely, think of the energy generated when people are able to maximize their talents.

- *on a person's health* when business strategy revolves entirely around profit, with little consideration for quality, service, people or ethics.

- *on organizational health* when promotions are based more on personal contacts than on team contributions, of systematic bias against certain groups of people, of pay and status unrelated to performance, or recognition that comes only when an employee does something wrong.

- *on a person's productivity* when insufficient training is provided to do the job, when managers don't know how to run effective meetings, or when creativity is not encouraged.

- *on organizational productivity* when plans are not communicated, when more effort is required to support bureaucracy than to get the "real job" done, or when it is difficult to get the information you need to do your job.

- *on people's health* when the values of the business are totally out of alignment with the values of employees or when the organization is perceived to perform no socially useful purpose.[3]

Lack of vision is not limited to the corporate world. For example, drug abuse is a bane of urban life and beyond. Poverty and homelessness are increasing, and the gap between the rich and poor has become more painfully obvious. Thirty seven million people in the United States are without health insurance; and the educational system is producing more functional illiterates than it ever has in the past. Organizations cannot divorce themselves from these issues or delude themselves that they are somehow immune. There are holes in the boat. Lounging in the captain's chambers will not secure survival.

Some companies, however, are *capitalizing* on ethical opportunities. They believe that human capital is a prepotent source of economic gain. Therefore, they are investing in the growth and retention of their valuable resources. They believe that when the customer wins, they win. Therefore, they are establishing interdependent relationships which result in mutual productivity and profitability. They believe that the earth one day will be one community—the only community. Therefore, they are looking for ways to safeguard and enhance the environment, not to exploit it.

Leaders need to check the inclusivity of their corporate vision statements by assessing the extent to which employees, customers and the community are represented. Specifically, they need to ensure that the vision represents the interdependent relationship between the company and its stakeholders, and reflects a belief that the company wins when employees, customers and the community wins.

Some examples of interdependent vision statements are:

"We win when the customer wins"

"Being 'Number 1' means doing the right thing all the time"

"We maximize our profits by maximizing customer profits".

Values

The Issues

In order to understand the "ethical edge," one must see the connection among vision, values and strategy. Understanding this connection requires a fundamental view that organizations consist of human beings, and that organizations consist of a variety of stakeholders in a variety of communities.[4] Thus, the behaviors and actions by individuals and organizations are a reflection of their values relative to people and communities. And the success of the organization is due in large measure to the choices and actions of all stakeholders in their respective communities. It is axiomatic, then, that corporate strategy must reflect an understanding of the values of organizational members and stakeholders and an understanding of the ethical nature of strategic choice.

Few organizations have articulated a well-defined set of values that serve as guidelines for decision making and as anchors in a "sea of change." However, in a review of the codes of conduct and mission statements of several organizations, these values seem to appear frequently:

PROFITS
QUALITY
INTEGRITY
RESPECT FOR INDIVIDUALS
RESPECT FOR CUSTOMERS
RESPECT FOR COMMUNITIES
FAIRNESS
HONESTY
EQUALITY OF OPPORTUNITY
OPENNESS
EMPOWERMENT
ATTRACTIVE AND SAFE WORKING CONDI-
    TIONS
COMPETITIVE COMPENSATION
CONFIDENTIALITY
PROTECTION OF THE ENVIRONMENT
COMPLIANCE WITH THE LAW
EDUCATION
INTERDEPENDENCE
JOB SATISFACTION
PERSONAL FULFILLMENT

More and more, organizations want to be clear about what values drive their decisions and influence their behavior. These organizations have found that it is critical to articulate and communicate these values to all employees in a variety of media on a frequent basis.

There are three problems related to articulating values. First, many people are uncomfortable about articulating values. They view the individual as the sole judge of what is right and wrong. This thinking leads to a personal and situational view of ethics, namely, "what I do is my business." In this kind of culture, it is difficult to confront people on values they may have that differ from the organization. In the book, *Habits of the Heart*, Bellah and his associates explore the dangers of rampant individualism in our society.[5]

Second, some organizations feel that roles determine values. For example, executives who feel it their duty as corporate citizens to achieve profit objectives independent of the effects on people, customers and the community satisfy one value while they violate several others. The whole notion that different levels of an organization have different privileges relative to morality must be challenged.

Third, some organizations believe that you can't change values. It's not practical. This belief leads to a "get along, go along" view of ethics. For example, many people in marketing are heard to say, "It's accepted practice to provide under-the-counter payments in this business. If you don't do it, you don't sell." Confronting the justification, "in this business, everyone does it," requires a great deal of courage— particularly in well-established subgroups where these problems are most likely to arise. In addition, the belief that values are ingrained and cannot be changed leads to a victimized view of ethics. For example, in South Africa apartheid is justified by its history and tradition. Companies who do business in South Africa may say, "Around here, that's just the way it is". Even though several companies abide by the Sullivan Principles, most blacks still feel foreign involvement in South Africa perpetuates apartheid. And Sullivan himself has since disowned his own principles, saying they proved ineffective. Dealing with these issues and responding to pressures from investors and employees for doing the right thing forces executives to look inside and decide if they are going to confront these issues.

The bottom line is that we must articulate our values with the belief that we will and can transform these values into the norms that define our organizational culture.

Norms

The Issues

The challenge of shaping the environment is our ability to transform our stated values into the norms which drive our organizations. This effort requires a systematic process of change. One system for changing an organizational culture is the 4D process (Diagnosis, Development, Delivery and Determination).

Every organization has strengths and weaknesses relative to its articulated values. Therefore, a culture-change effort must begin with an accurate diagnosis. This diagnosis begins with determining the employee perceptions of values and norms within the organization. Meetings with employees formally and informally at every level in the organization and gathering data through surveys are two of the methodologies that can be utilized to find out where a company stands relative to the stated values. The level of commitment of top management to these values must be unconditional if a culture-change effort is going to succeed. Many culture change efforts fail because the articulation of values is nothing more than an empty exercise to produce a proclamation. Some companies utilize a bottom-up approach in articulating the values, while other companies use a top-down approach. Independent of the approach, it is critical to learn about employees' perceptions of how important the values are to them; whether or not they are really norms in the organization; and if they getting better or worse. The result of the diagnosis is a comprehensive understanding of which values are strong or weak relative to the existing culture. In addition, the diagnosis should provide information on the perceived commitment and capacity of the organization to transform weak norms into strong norms.

Following the diagnosis comes the development phase of the change effort. Effective and lasting change requires a broad base of leadership skills and support within the organization. Development includes four activities.

- *Communication.* Sharing the results of the organizational diagnosis and explaining the effect of culture on organizational behavior, personal performance and business objectives.

- *Involvement.* Ensuring that activities aimed at increasing commitment and enhancing capacity occur with the participation of people from all appropriate levels. Often, involvement takes the form of cross-functional task forces and teams.

- *Skills Enhancement.* Usually there is a requirement to improve the leadership skills, relating skills, thinking skills and change agent skills of key players in the organization who will lead the change effort.

- *Planning.* Setting specific goals and time lines for changing the organizational norms is a requirement. Planning means deciding how the changes and goals will be implemented. In some cases, that might mean continuation of specific task forces, or modifying the organizational structure, or giving additional responsibilities to existing functions.

Many culture-change efforts fail because they treat diagnosis or development as the goal line. Perhaps the most difficult part of any change effort for most organizations is the delivery and implementation of the plans that are developed. Delivery includes those activities specifically aimed at increasing commitment, enhancing capacity and mobilizing support for leaders and employees. The principles of effective delivery include leadership role-modeling; rewards and recognition for desired behavior; ongoing discussion of the vision, values and goals of the change effort; and feedback on results achievement.

Leadership modeling behavior sets the tone for the culture. People take their cues from their leaders, whether these cues are implicit or explicit. The case of Oliver North, a central figure in the Iran-Contra controversy in the U.S. in the late 1980s, demonstrates

---

that fact well. Colonel North may not have had explicit directions to operate above the law, but his actions were implicitly encouraged. A wink and a nod can send a powerful message through the culture. And the fact that North could make the assumption that his superiors approved of his dangerous activities says a great deal about the leadership and the culture.

In addition, reward systems must be designed to reinforce desired behaviors in the culture. There are very few organizational cultures in which managers are called into the executive suite to be applauded or chastised for their ethics. For example, think of the last time you heard of any organizational president calling a special meeting to recognize a manager for supporting personal growth. And recognition should not be limited to one individual. The reward system should provide opportunities for peers to recognize the extent to which employees adhere to desired norms in the culture. Unless ethical behaviors are included in performance reviews, they will not be viewed as important as other behaviors that may result in short term profits but long term disaster.

Communications must be ongoing. In his book *Thriving on Chaos,* Tom Peters implores leaders to become the vision's foremost itinerant preacher. Peters suggests, "Do not let a single day pass without taking at least two or three opportunities to deliver your three-minute stump speech on the vision and to showcase events and people (small events and front-line people) that are illustrative of initiatives which support the vision."[6] Desired norms need to be constantly recognized and reinforced through a variety of communication vehicles.

The final phase of the 4D process is determination. Determination represents a return to the diagnostic phase of the 4D process. Effective change is an ongoing cycle of exploration, understanding and action. Exploration of where we *are* leads to an understanding of where we need to *go*, and acting on that understanding gets us to the goal line. The important principles of determination are that it builds on what has been accomplished, and it continues the change process.

Essentially, constructive corporate cultural change means creating positive norms that influence ethical behavior. These norms can best be understood in terms of "around hereisms." For example, in an ethical culture, a norm might be "Around here, we don't accept gifts from vendors," or "Around here, we don't use inside information to our own advantage."

In many instances of unethical behavior it is easy to attribute all the blame to deficiencies in the individual character or to greed, but rarely is that the whole story. For instance, what were the norms in those organizations that encouraged, permitted, accepted, rewarded or tolerated unethical behaviors? How much of the problem was cultural and how much was individual? Clearly, individuals must assume responsibility for their own behavior and be held accountable. But organizations must also ask the hard questions that arise concerning the environment in which individuals work if they are going to be successful in shaping the kind of environment they want.

According to David Grier, Vice-President at the Royal Bank of Canada, "There is a fundamental difference between developing an ethical corporate policy . . . and making sure that employees don't lie, steal, cheat, discriminate, engage in sexual harassment etc." He goes on to say that:

"Many business people haven't thought this difference through and many corporate codes of ethics don't seem to reflect this difference. Many talk a lot about what is required of employees, without saying very much about the conduct and obligations the corporation requires of itself.

"From the ethical perspective, the foundation has to be shared values. If the value system of a company is not tended and is not continually re-expressed and renewed, and it is not backed up by strategies, structures, and systems designed to bring it into actual practice, then it will become mere lip service.

"It is persistent effort to ensure consistent application of the values in the development of strategy, structure and systems, and a solid coherence between them that is most likely to secure the commitment of staff. In other words, a positive ethical perspective has to be built into the whole warp and woof of business management." (*Globe and Mail,* December 13, 1989, p. B2.)

Once again, it is the authors' belief that the corporate culture defines the ways in which an organization treats its employees, its customers and its community. In an ethical culture, people are assisted in obtaining fulfillment in their jobs; customers are seen as interdependent partners; and the community is viewed as a resource to be enhanced.

Unfortunately, realigning corporate culture is not an easy task. The 4D process outlined above can be a potent methodology for helping executives through the change process. It must be remembered though, that even with a strong commitment and an effective process, successful culture change efforts take anywhere from three to five years. Yet, our experience clearly demonstrates that a commitment to create an ethical culture positively impacts the organization even in its earliest stages.

Exemplars

Some mainstream exemplars in the area of corporate culture include such giants as IBM, Four Seasons Hotels, Levi Strauss and Co. and Delta Airlines. IBM, with 450,000 employees and $60 Billion in annual revenues is famous, among other characteristics, for its innovative and compassionate means of reducing its work force by thousands of employees without compromising its "no lay off" policy. Respect for the individual, attrition, early retirement and retraining have been used at great expense to the company.

Four Seasons Hotel, the World's leading luxury hotel operator, has partially created its leading edge through its human resources practices and its treatment of workers in a traditionally low paying industry.

Levi Strauss and Company of San Francisco is a well known leader in corporate philanthropy. It is distinguised by its unusual effort to get employees to take ownership of charitable contributions by having them decide where a large portion of the philanthropic budget goes. Famous for not laying off its people, Delta Airlines has established a unique relationship with its employees. As a token of their appreciation for Delta's commitment to people, the employees chipped in and bought a 727 airplane for the company. This type of relationship is extraordinary given the absence of loyalty in so many corporations.

These examples all speak to the relationship between ethics and financial performance. In terms of profits, market share and efficiency, these companies are all leaders in their industries. And they are ethical exemplars as well.

Challenge

Creating an ethical culture means empowering people through investments in human and information capital and instilling employees with a passion for integrity. As such, culture change is the prepotent factor in ethical enhancement. If an organization were able to create and sustain an ethical culture, then the way it deals with people, with customers and with communities would be fairly automatic. The ethical organization simply does the right thing.

The key principles for achieving an ethical culture are to create an ideal vision of the ethical organization, define the values that anchor that vision, and shape an environment that transforms the values into norms so that the ideal can eventually be achieved. This chapter discusses the issues related to each of those principles and provides exemplars of organizations that have created an ethical culture.

The challenge to ethical leaders is to ask the hard questions before they act. In today's fast-paced and fast-changing business world, where time is seen as a competitive weapon, executives are vulnerable to leaving the hard questions unaddressed and unanswered. In order to create an ethical culture, leaders must invest their time in the vision, values and norms that give people a sense of pride in their organizations.

CHAPTER TWO

WINNING THROUGH PEOPLE

Introduction

It is very common in organizations to talk about people as the most valuable and valued asset, but it is very uncommon to see a consistent set of actions and initiatives which support that statement. In most organizations, that phrase is simply an empty slogan that causes more cynicism than satisfaction.

Dealing ethically with people means more than having a fair compensation system. Instead, it involves consideration of a person's physical, emotional, intellectual and spiritual needs. Physically, those needs might include compensation, safe and healthy working conditions, and a pleasant environment. Emotionally, those needs might include respect, involvement, teamwork and consideration for family issues. Intellectually, those needs might include opportunities for growth, training, variety and support for personal development. And spiritually, those needs might include a sense of community, connectedness and purpose.

An ethical organization is driven to treat its employees as ends and not merely as a means for generating profits. An ethical organization understands the principle of human capital. In the information age, human resources become more valuable only if they are developed. Therefore, strengthening the connection between profits and the development of people achieves ethical goals as well as traditional business objectives.

Overview

Vision

Winning through people means treating employees as whole persons with unique values, differences and needs.

These are the assumptions related to the connection between profits and treating people right. When employees are treated right,

- they are seen as more than "pairs of hands";
- recruitment and retention efforts are enhanced;
- productivity and morale are improved;
- more constructive, interdependent relationships are formed.
- quality, innovation and teamwork all improve.

Principles

Winning through people requires a multifaceted approach which must include:

1. *Developing* employees in ways that increase their productivity and market value.
2. *Promoting* health and safety.
3. *Supporting* a sense of balance in employees' lives.
4. *Valuing* differences.

Rating scale for winning through people

The following scale will help you assess where you are, and set goals for the people-oriented dimension of your business.

5.0 Become an exemplar for winning through people.

4.0 Create a culture that nurtures personal and professional growth through, for instance, innovative performance management and succession planning.

3.0 Provide proactive people programs, such as day care, employee assistance and health promotion programs.

2.0 Comply with the law by observing Equal Employment Opportunity (EEO) requirements.

1.0 Stay out of trouble with people; for example, avoid labor relations problems.

For specific scales on each of the aspects, refer to Appendix A.

Employee Development

The Issues

The ethical challenge for all companies is to create an educational core of generic skills for all employees. The ethical advantage requires the creation of new psychological contracts with employees, in which employers empower workers with skills which increase their street value. It also requires that employees contribute to the organization through improved functional applications which improve the company's competitive advantage. Since 85 percent of economic productivity growth is a result of the synergistic interaction of human and information capital[1,2], it makes sense to invest in people and their ideas. In short, the investment in education is sound from an ethical as well as economic perspective. It is the area that not only yields the best return on investment but also causes the most problems when poorly done or not done at all.

It is generally agreed that North America faces a triple-deficit threat: The trade deficit, the budget deficit, and the education deficit. While the first two are frightening, the third could be disastrous. By the time North American students graduate from high school, they rank last among the top 15 industrialized nations.[3] If this situation continues, and we remain in last place among the "informationalized" countries, the competitive position of North American industry will be jeopardized.

The skill gap is widening rapidly. Requirements in the information age are accelerating for technically skilled, computer-literate people. And the pool of skilled talent is drying up. The school systems are just one factor in this issue. There are sociological influences as well. The report, *Workforce 2000,* prepared by the Hudson Institute, a New York think tank, projects that 85 percent of new job applicants will consist of minorities, immigrants and women.[4] This work force will have a wide variety of educational needs. Thus, the trade deficit and the budget deficit, as serious as

they are, are dwarfed in significance by the educational deficit.

The Wall Street Journal reports that work-force
shortages of the 1990s may accomplish what the ac-
tivism of the 1960s couldn't: that is, plunge corporations deeply into social issues.[5] And companies can't
afford to take a wait-and-see approach. If they do,
warns Samuel Ehrenhalt, a commissioner with the
U.S. Bureau of Labor Statistics, they risk being left
without enough capable employees in the the not-too-
distant future. In work force terms, the year 2000
began in the fall of 1989. That's when the graduating
class of 2000 entered first grade.

One fear is that, increasingly, the workers available
to do a given job won't be able to handle it. The Hudson Institute predicts that 41 percent of jobs created
through the end of the century will be "high-skill" ones,
versus 24 percent currently. Yet many new workers
lack even basic job skills.[6] Thus, companies must edu-
cate for productivity and for life.

From a business point of view, another fear is that
development investments will be wasted because
people will learn and leave. And competitors who
don't invest in people development will thus be able to
afford higher salaries to attract "educated" people.
The other side of that issue, however, is that the companies which develop employees will create an image
of a desired employer. As values shift and "making a
life" becomes as important as "making a living," educa-
tionally oriented companies will attract the best talent.
It is also unlikely that the best educated members of

the work force will gravitate toward organizations that do not invest in people.

Health and Safety

The Issues

The effect of work on an employee's health and well-being is an ethical issue of major proportions. While most organizations see health as a responsibility and as a tool for preventing losses, few see it as a vehicle for enhancing individual productivity and organizational health.

Some progressive companies, however, have realized significant returns on investment from their health promotion efforts. Johnson & Johnson, AT&T, and Control Data Corporation all report at least a $2 return for every $1 invested in comprehensive health enhancement programs.[7,8,9] These companies were motivated to make significant investments not only because of their belief that health promotion would contribute to the human capital of the firm, but also because it appeared to be the best strategy for containing health care costs.

As most executives know, health care costs are rising astronomically. In the U.S., the total health care bill exceeded $600 billion in 1989, more than 12 percent of the Gross National Product (GNP). Employers paid almost 30% of that cost in direct health care expenses. Those costs can be translated into direct effects on the bottom line. In 1987, employee health care expenses equalled an average of 94.2 percent of after-tax corporate profits in America.[10] And these costs are rising at 15–20 percent per year—a rate of increase almost four times that of the Consumer Price Index.[11] If this rate continues, health care costs will soon overtake corporate profits altogether.

If those figures are not enough, the Prudential Insurance Company of New York determined costs to be $500,000 in recruiting and retraining a replacement for a high-level executive who dies from a heart attack at age 50. In addition, an estimated 60–70 percent of all employee insurance claims arise from such problems as smoking, obesity and alcoholism.[12] Indeed, more than 50 percent of all illnesses are lifestyle related, which means they can be prevented.[13] And these are just the economic costs. The human costs may be even more significant.

Safety is an ethical issue because the way an organization treats this issue demonstrates how committed they are to fundamental human considerations and employee rights. Like the cost of quality, there is definitely a cost associated with the effectiveness of accident prevention efforts. Most companies do not have a system that identifies the magnitude of this cost; consequently, they have difficulty with attempts to prioritize safety needs against other demands on limited resources.

The consequences of accidental events can be segregated into two major categories; human and economic. While the human category is of major concern, one must also look at the economic aspects to ensure proper allocation of resources.

Examples of costs that fall into the economic category are: workers compensation, property damage, wage subsidies to injured workers, overtime costs, increased supervisory time, lost efficiency, production downtime, extra hiring costs, training costs, and others.

National averages and industry studies provide us with the following insights:

The average cost of a disabling injury. (This cost includes: workers compensation, insurance, wages, medical expense, insurance administration but does not include property damage): $16,500

The average number of property loss incidents an organization will incur for every disabling injury: 30

The range of dollars lost in property damage (without injury) for every dollar lost due to disabling injuries: $5–50[14,15]

Keeping these averages in mind, consider a corporation's potential costs assuming 500 lost-time accidents in a year.

The probable dollar loss the corporation incurred due to disabling injuries = $8.2 Million ($16,500 x 500)

The potential number of property damage Incidents for 1988: 15,000 (30 x 500).

The potential range of dollars lost in property damage due to accidental events: $41 Million to $410 Million ($5.0–$50.00 x $8.2 Million)

These numbers make the case that taking an ethical approach to safety is not only the right thing to do, it is also an economic imperative.

Another important factor is the increased regulatory activity over the past decade that has been focused on workplace safety. This has been prompted mainly by a heightened public awareness and concern brought about by a series of industrial catastrophes.

As well, the variety of hazardous materials in most industrial operations warrants concern. And most organizations are having difficulties in complying with new legislative requirements because they often do not have access to information related to the purchase, receipt, storage, dispensing and replacement of these materials.

Leaders who are genuinely interested in winning the right way recognize the fundamental importance of health and safety. The building blocks for organizational development are analogous to Abraham Maslow's hierarchy for individual development. Just as food and shelter must be secured before a person has a reasonable chance to aspire toward a feeling of belonging, self-esteem, and self-actualization, health and safety issues need to be addressed before an organization can aspire to higher levels of organizational development. For ethical reasons and for business reasons, enlightened leaders promote the health and safety of their employees.

Supporting Balance

The Issues

Employees are more and more determined to pursue interests that go beyond the job. And employers are recognizing that multidimensional people add value to their businesses. It makes sense, therefore, from a human and economic point of view, to support balance in people's lives.

In a 1987 poll of 50,000 employees, American Telephone and Telegraph Co. (AT&T) found that its work force was interested in more than salaries.[16] The survey revealed a growing concern among employees, more than half of them women, about tending to their families, particularly young children.

On May 28, 1989, AT&T reached agreement with two of the largest unions representing AT&T workers on a three-tier contract covering 175,000 people. Both sides described the agreement as groundbreaking in its handling of a wide range of personal, family and child care issues. Among the novel provisions are the creation of a $5-million fund, provided by AT&T, to develop community child care centers and services for the elderly; grants of up to $2,000 to cover adoption costs; and an extension of unpaid parental leave.

Herb Linnen, AT&T Director of Media Relations, says, "We are now looking into the 1990s, and we realize that to compete nationally and globally, we have to attract the best people and keep them. An overriding factor is the degree to which you can relieve some of that family worry."[17]

AT&T's family care package included a variety of benefits that company and union representatives say have never before been included in a union contract covering such a large number of workers. Although some major corporations such as IBM include child care in their benefits, no large union has ever succeeded in making this a subject of negotiations.[18]

The Conference Board of Canada surveyed 385 companies with a total of approximately 1.1 million employees and found that demographic, social and economic changes are leading employers to reassess policies aimed at recruiting and retaining employees. The Board discovered that companies are responding to personal and family needs in a variety of innovative ways. Most common is offering more flexible work schedules. Nearly 30 percent offer part-time work with prorated benefits, more than 25 percent offer compressed weeks, almost 20 percent offer job sharing. And a few companies are beginning to offer specific support for employees with children.[19] Companies are beginning to build into their value systems the understanding that they "share" the responsibility for the employees' economic as well as emotional well-being. For example, Johnson & Johnson has embarked on a new program that makes an employee's personal concerns a matter of corporate concern by involving the managment proactively in allowing employees time-off (with pay) to address short-term stress inducing problems, such as child care, elder care, family substance abuse, and others.

As the workplace and the work force continue to change, a new set of values may emerge and the relative importance of certain values may shift. If current trends continue, employees will have an increasing desire to attend to family needs and personal development goals. The obvious danger is that employees may find themselves unable to cope with family and personal concerns due to mounting workplace stress levels. And this threatens to impair workplace productivity. Ethical leaders will respond to these changes by supporting balance in a person's life.

Valuing Differences

The Issues

As *Workforce 2000* becomes a reality (85 percent of new entrants consisting of women, minorities and immigrants), the ways in which companies recognize and involve these new populations and value the inherent differences among their employees will play a major role in the companies' success.

Of 92 companies that participated in an independently sponsored Equal Employment Opportunity (EEO) study in 1986, 47 had at least one representative of a minority group on their board. Among these, 39 had one, 7 had two, and one company, forest-products giant Kimberly Clark Corporation, had three. Of the 81 companies that provided information on minorities in top management, 29 reported at least one minority officer, with 16 having one, 8 with two, 2 with three, and Coca-Cola, ITT Corporation and Marriott Corporation with four each.[20]

According to Catalyst, a New York based organization that focuses on career and family issues for women, there were only 46 women serving on boards of directors of the *Fortune* 1350 in 1969 (3 percent). By 1985, the number had grown to 339 serving on 407 boards of the *Fortune* 1000 (41 percent), and by 1986, the number had risen to 395 women on 439 boards (44 percent). A substantially lower percentage of companies reported women in top management positions. Even IBM, which has a solid reputation for ensuring equal opportunities for women and blacks, did not promote its first woman to the vice-presidential level until 1985.[21]

Among the most frequent complaints of women and minorities working their way up the corporate ladder is that they are channeled into staff rather than line positions. Staff positions typically are not on a career track leading to the office of the chief executive. Even at this writing, the only *Fortune* 500 firm headed by a female CEO is *The Washington Post*, run by Katherine Graham, who is its majority shareholder.

These surveys show how business firms responded when they came under pressure in the 1960s to expand corporate governance to include greater numbers of women and ethnic minorities. Many businesses responded by adding a women director to the board, resulting in an observable increase in the number of companies with at least one woman director.[22] In spite of these initial responses, however, more than 50 percent of the *Fortune* 1000 still have no women directors; and women hold only 3 to 4 percent of the total *Fortune* 1000 directorships[23] and 2 percent of the officerships,[24] despite the fact that women have entered the workplace in unprecedented numbers.[25] At the same time, less than 2 percent of the director-ships are likely to be held by minorities.[26] And less than 1 percent of the 1362 corporate officers surveyed in 1985 were minorities.[27]

As Third World and Eastern European markets continue to open, radical changes will be forced on companies competing in global markets. Even now, major high technology companies, such as Digital Equipment Corp., IBM, and Prime Computer, Inc., generate more than 50 percent of their revenues from the non-U.S. marketplace.

The closed, male dominated system will have to adapt for its own survival, and minorities, females and recent immigrant groups will represent much of the creative efforts needed for companies to achieve global preeminence. These groups will be demanding that their values and approaches to the marketplace be given recognition and credence.

Exemplars

An ethical exemplar in the area of people is Herman Miller, Inc., the second-largest U.S. manufacturer of office furniture, based near Grand Rapids, Michigan. Herman Miller, Inc. which had $793 million in sales in the fiscal year 1989, was the first to introduce the "open office concept" in the early 1960s. It has been called one of the most admired companies by *Fortune* magazine.[28]

Max De Pree, chairman of Herman Miller, Inc., bases his management philosophy on the idea that nobody is common; every employee has a right to be an insider. De Pree has summarized his business philosophy in terms of sharing: "Capitalism can only reach its potential when it capitalizes on all workers' gifts and lets them share in the results." Two years ago, De Pree began to write down his thoughts about management. The result is a book called *Leadership is an Art.*[29] Material from that book will be summarized here to demonstrate why Herman Miller, Inc. was selected as an exemplar for the people section of this book.

De Pree begins by defining the art of leadership as liberating people to do what is required of them in the most effective and humane way possible. In "The Millwright Died," the first chapter of the book, De Pree captures the essence of dealing ethically with people.

> My father is ninety-six years old. He is the founder of Herman Miller, and much of the value system and impounded energy of the company, a legacy still drawn on today, is a part of his contribution. In the furniture industry of the 1920s the machines of most factories were not run by electric motors, but by pulleys from a central drive shaft. The central drive shaft was run by the steam engine. The steam engine got it steam from the boiler. The boiler, in our case, got its fuel from the sawdust and other waste coming out of the machine room—a beautiful cycle.
>
> The millwright was the person who oversaw that cycle and on whom the entire activity of the operation depended. He was a key person.

One day the millwright died.

My father, being a young manager at the time, did not particularly know what he should do when a key person died, but thought he ought to go visit the family. He went to the house and was invited to join the family in the living room. There was some awkward conversation—the kind with which many of us are familiar.

The widow asked my father if it would be all right if she read aloud some poetry. Naturally, he agreed. She went into another room, came back with a bound book, and for many minutes read selected pieces of beautiful poetry. When she finished, my father commented on how beautiful the poetry was and asked who wrote it. She replied that her husband, the millwright, was the poet.

It is now nearly sixty years since the millwright died, and my father and many of us at Herman Miller continue to wonder: Was he a poet who did millwright's work, or was he a millwright who wrote poetry?

In our effort to understand corporate life, what is it we should learn from this story? In addition to all of the ratios and goals and parameters and bottom lines, it is fundamental that leaders endorse a concept of persons. This begins with an understanding of the diversity of people's gifts and talents and skills.

Understanding and accepting diversity enables us to see that each of us is needed. It also enables us to begin to think about being abandoned to the strengths of others, of admitting that we cannot *know* or *do* everything.

The simple act of recognizing diversity in corporate life helps us to connect the great variety of gifts that people bring to the work and service of the organization. Diversity allows each of us to contribute in a special way, to make our special gift a part of the corporate effort.

Recognizing diversity helps us to understand the need we have for opportunity, equity, and identity in the workplace. Recognizing diversity gives us the chance to provide meaning, fulfillment, and purpose, which are not to be relegated solely to private life any more than are such things as love, beauty, and joy. It also helps us to undersand that for many of us there is a fundamental difference between goals and rewards.

In the end, diversity is not only real in our corporate groups but, as with the millwright, it frequently goes unrecognized.

Max De Pree began with a poetic story about a poet. He goes on with what a leader owes his organization. Specifically, he says, leaders owe:

- Vital financial health, and the relationship and reputation that enable continuity of that financial health.
- A clear statement of the values of the organization.
- A new reference point for what caring, purposeful, commited people can be in the institutional setting.
- A certain maturity.

- Rationality.
- A sense of freedom to its people.

According to De Pree, a leader can tell the difference between "living edges" and "dying" ones. To lose sight of the beauty of ideas and of hope and opportunity, and to frustrate the right to be needed, is to be at the dying edge.

To be a part of a throwaway mentality that discards goods and ideas, that discards principles and law, that discards persons and families, is to be at the dying edge.

To be at the leading edge of consumption, affluence, and instant gratification is to be at the dying edge.

To ignore the dignity of work and the elegance of simplicity, and the essential responsibilty of serving others, is to be at the dying edge.

To be a leader (on the living edge) means having the opportunity to make a meaningful difference in the lives of those who permit leaders to lead.

Challenge

While this chapter covers several key topic areas, the main point is that winning through people means treating individuals as whole persons with unique physical, emotional, intellectual and spiritual needs, values and differences. Ethical leadership revolves around four key principles: developing employees, promoting health and safety, supporting balance and valuing differences.

The first challenge to the ethical executive is to confront deficiencies in each of those fundamental areas and to fix them. Beyond the initial challenge, the ethical leader, who is committed to winning through people, will have four major goals:

- to inspire people through the vision and values
- to empower people with skills and support
- to build teamwork through cross-functional interdependence
- to free people to initiate through responsibility and authority

Accomplishing these difficult challenges will require trememendous dedication, but will clearly communicate to employees that they are the key resources in the organization.

CHAPTER THREE

WINNING WITH CUSTOMERS

Introduction

Customers demand more from their suppliers than ever before. They demand the highest quality products at the lowest possible price. They demand that products are customized to meet their unique needs. They demand that products and services are delivered in accordance with requirements just in time all the time. They demand immediate and excellent service when problems or concerns arise. In the age of abundance, we expect these demands from our customers. They are a given. If we don't meet the demands, a competitor will.

But a new set of expectations are emerging from customers, expectations that many companies may not be prepared to meet. These new expectations revolve around customer's demand for integrity, interdependence and growth. Customers are disgusted by manipulation and impatient with surveys probing their satisfaction. And often they are suspicious about who benefits in "partnership" and "immersion" relationships.

Dealing ethically with customers is one of the best strategies for responding to the new set of customer expectations. The rub is that ethics, by definition, cannot be a clever, new manipulation game. It has to be real. This chapter explores the ingredients for customer success in the area of integrity.

Overview

Vision

Winning with customers means conducting all interactions with the highest levels of integrity and interdependence.

These are the assumptions that strengthen the connection between profits and customer ethics: Companies that treat customers right:

- create interdependent relationships in which both parties realize productivity and profitability gains;
- establish their organization as a preferred provider in a customer world increasingly concerned with ethics;
- improve employee pride in the organization;
- heighten the importance of ethics in all transactions.

Principles

Winning with customers is a multidimensional approach which must incorporate:

1. Thinking about customer benefits before **product development**.
2. Ensuring customer safety when **producing/ manufacturing** products.
3. Relating constructively and honestly with customers while **marketing** the product.

4. Insisting on fairness toward customers when **distributing and servicing** the product.

Rating scale for winning with customers

The following scale will help you determine where you are and where you want to be.

5.0 Interdependent relationships with customers

4.0 Immersion in the customer's business

3.0 An obsession with customer benefits

2.0 A passion for customer satisfaction

1.0 An orientation toward customer manipulation

A discussion of this five-level scale is contained in Appendix A.

Product Development

The Issues

The creation of the atomic bomb is a dramatic example of how ethical issues are important in the early stages of any product development activity. Now, of course, with new advances in DNA research and biogenetic engineering, ethical issues are constantly arising. To create a forum to address the medical aspects of these types of conflicts, the Hastings Center was established. The Hastings Center is a New York-based nonprofit, nonpartisan organization that carries out educational and research programs on ethical issues in medicine, the life sciences and the professions. It was formed to explore biomedical ethics issues.

On a more general level, most companies have ethical issues that arise in relation to their products. For example, research shows that 1,000 people die every day as a result of smoking cigarettes.[1] And yet, tobacco industries still hire consultants to help them find creative ways to get adolescents to smoke. What sort of ethical conflicts must this present for the employees who work in these industries or for consultants who charge them fees for clever advertising ideas. As we move into the next century, increasing numbers of employees will want to know about the types of products that the hiring company produces and the process by which it resolves ethical issues surrounding those products.

Product safety scored an impressive comeback as a political issue in the 1960s after a period of dormancy during and following World War II.[2] The tragedies that arose from design deficiencies with the drug Thalidomide and the Corvair sports car (the subject of Ralph Nader's first book, *Unsafe at Any Speed*), were instrumental in reawakening public interest. And the growing technological content, performance expectations, and potency of many products appear to have increased the risk and hazard of malfunction.[3]

Public demands in this area have become more complicated and serious for the corporation because the degree of liability attibuted to the manufacturer for the use of its products has increased. There appears to be a deterioration in the manufacturer's legal position caused by a tendency to hold the manufacturer liable for injury regardless of negligence on its part.[4] The issue here isn't the wanton issuing of lawsuits that may have no grounds for success, but the willingness of government and the courts to legislate or, in the case of judges, reinterpret the law to punish companies.

In this context, the product development function is heavily influenced by four major issues: public interest, quality assurance, ecology and solid waste. Each will be briefly discussed below.

Public interest advocates have placed products under increasing scrutiny for performance, design standards and product composition. This surveillance has resulted in product recalls, public warnings, and customer refunds which frequently entail considerable expense and loss of sales. For example, automobile recalls to correct a single defect can cost tens of millions of dollars.

The impact of quality assurance on product development is also substantial. Product engineers are now expected to understand the circumstances in which a product will be used and misused, anticipate the effects of aging and changing conditions on its performance, and incorporate these factors in product specifications. Product design engineers are expected to meet performance and cost criteria while being cognizant of recognized potential social demands. And in an increasingly technological age, executives must also consider the downside potential of using technology for destructive purposes. For example, phones can now be programmed to ring busy for selected numbers. Should phone manufacturers provide the software that will enable consumers to prevent access from "undesirable" people?

The product development function is also influenced by ecological considerations. This concern has achieved global prominence because of the destruction of the ozone layer and widespread concerns about the greenhouse effect. The most visible example of this has been the controversy over automobile exhaust emissions, originally established in the 1970 U.S. Clean Air Act amendments. These regulations are becoming even more stringent and may result in the battery-powered cars in the near future.

The solid waste issue is still another concern effecting product development. Consumption of packaging materials amounts to millions of tons a year in North America. As landfill capacity continues to shrink, litter becomes less tolerated, and resource shortages become more severe, there will be increasing pressure to attend to this issue in the product development phase. From the corporate perspective, the waste disposal issue has led to the development of a greater interest in utilizing recycled materials in the manufacturing process and the redesign of products to minimize the eventual disposal difficulty.[5]

The difficulty in applying ethical standards to product development is that advancements in technology may demonstrate potentially harmful effects that could not be anticipated. What happens when innocent and honest efforts to produce a product are called into question by new research? Should companies who engage in responsible research suffer the same liabilities as companies that forge ahead with little thought?

Manufacturing

The Issues

The Industrial Revolution effected three important changes in manufacturing. First, mechanization diminished the need for skilled craftsmen. Second, the increased volume of production required standardized procedures and precluded close personal interaction between owners and workers. And third, industrialization required people not only to work outside of their homes, but usually to relocate from rural communities into urban areas. These changes dramatically affected social relations and moral values.[6]

The current Age of Information has dramatically reversed all three changes. First, technological advances have increased the need for highly skilled labor or "knowledge workers" as management guru Peter Drucker calls them. Second, the notion of customization for adding value to specific client needs has demanded high levels of information processing (resulting in a transformation within manufacturing from procedures to processing); and then relating the resultant ideas in constructive ways with peers and supervisors (which means a transformation from depersonalization to personalization). And third, computerization has made it possible for people to work on the same project simultaneously at a multitude of locations.

The management theory that emerged out of the Industrial Revolution was primarily embodied by *The Principles of Scientific Management* (1911.) The primary author of this theory, American engineer Frederick Taylor, expressed the belief that most workers tended to work too slowly, making any system based on a worker's initiative inefficient.[7] Since Taylor considered human individuality cumbersome, he shaped a standardized work system that made employees replaceable, like the parts of a machine. He divided the work process into thinking and acting—managers did the former while workers did the latter.

In contrast to Taylor's mechanistic approach to management, the Hawthorne studies conducted in the 1930s at Western Electric[8] suggested that worker groups had their own values, norms of behavior and informal systems. The study demonstrated inadvertently that productivity increased when a work situation was constantly attended to and stimulated, regardless of the type of intervention—lights up, productivity up; lights down, productivity up again. But, more importantly, this approach viewed employees as members of a social system and attempted to understand how they were motivated within this context.[9]

Out of this historical background, the information age has emerged and demanded an evolution of the way we think of the manufacturing process. As a result, production managers and process engineers have been beset by demands that they adopt a more inclusive definition of environmental impact in the design and operation of production processes.[10] The manufacturing problem as it relates to ethics is manifested in three ways: degradation of the environment, of the health and safety of the workplace and of the quality of life of employees directly involved in the manufacturing process. Each of those impact areas will be briefly discussed below.

Although environmental control requirements may not have catastrophic consequences for all companies, the impact on the production function in several industries is significant. In some cases, regulations cannot be met with available control technology,[11] but significant progress has been made on a number of fronts to conquer the technological obstacles related to environmental protection. And the U.S. Environmental Protection Agency (EPA) has taken considerable pains to reduce economic dislocation likely to arise from requirements for more stringent efforts to prevent ecological damage. For example, as recently as 1975, the steel industry had not developed a practical means of abating air pollution in the coking process, nor had electric utilities been successful in devising methods of reducing sulfur oxide emissions in ways that were technically viable and economically feasible. By 1990, however, significant progress had been made on those issues.

Since regulations and compliance schedules generally impose deadlines, pressure is often exerted for early experimentation with new equipment. This process can be time-consuming, disruptive and expensive. Yet unwillingness to experiment may delay the start-up of new facilities or threaten shutdowns of existing ones with the attendant loss of jobs and capacity. And broader changes in raw materials, processes,

and products may also be dictated by ecological pressures. Thus, the expense of treating the noxious cook-
ing liquor residues in paper mills employing a sulfite
pulping process (once the dominant process in the industry) has contributed to the adoption of the kraft
process in new mills.[12]

The second major impact on the manufacturing
process, working conditions, has received increased
attention since the passage of the U.S. Occupational
Safety and Health Act (OSHA) in 1970. Some of the
most recent concerns relate to cumulative trauma dis-
orders, asbestos exposure, and disabling accidents.
And there is an ongoing need to attend to possible im-
pairments to health from sustained exposure to noise,
heat, dust, silica, carbon monoxide, and a host of
other process-related conditions.

The third impact on the manufacturing process,
quality of life issues, seems to be experiencing the
steepest upward trend in terms of its importance to
workers. As we have moved out of the "Tayloresque"
notions of manufacturing, through the Hawthorne ex-
periments and into the information age, employees'
needs and values have changed. As a result, manufacturing processes need to consider the issues that
affect employee well-being.

Marketing

The Issues

Many of the ethical issues facing companies today
are related not to the product itself, but to the manner

in which it is marketed and serviced. These issues can be categorized as follows: advertising and packaging; selling practices of the vendor; and product and performance warranties stipulated in the sales agreement. Each will be discussed briefly below.

Just as the manufacturing process has regulatory bodies to scrutinize its operations (such as the EPA and OSHA), advertising and packaging are monitored by the Federal Trade Commission. Since its creation in 1914, the main decree of this agency has been to prohibit "unfair methods of competition." As one might guess, deceptive advertising and packaging have been at the top of the FTC's list of abuses. Since television commands such a large share of the typical consumer's day, malpractice in this media is under close review. Essentially, companies are prohibited from deceptive use of research studies, unsubstantiated claims, inadequate disclosure, and deceptive television demonstration. Given the amount of advertising on food products, it appears that many companies have decided to push the limits of the law to its extreme. For example, claims are constantly made concerning the nutrition value of certain breakfast cereals or the low cholesterol content of particular foods when, in fact, the message is quite misleading.

Selling practices of vendors have a long history of consumer complaint. Exemplified by the proverbial snake oil salesman, the culprits have often been marginal characters who fraudulently foisted their goods and services on a gullible public. The movie *Tin Man* captures the modern day essence of the snake oil salesmen reincarnated as an aluminum siding vendor.

An extreme case of fraudulent misrepresentation was that of the Holland Furnace Company whose salesmen visited homeowners sometimes in the guise of "safety inspectors." Not wanting to be "accessories to murder" they offered to have the family furnace replaced. One salesman performed his duties so adroitly that an elderly woman purchased nine furnaces in six years at a cost of $18,000.[13]

In the 1980s, the boom of new, get-rich schemes coupled with advances in telemarketing produced a plethora of high pressure sales tactics. Financial advisors, credentialled only by their calling card, implored thousands of people to invest in tax-shelters, limited partnerships, and sure-fire stocks that in many cases turned sour and caused significant hardship, if not bankruptcy, for the consumers.

Finally, the issue of warranties has caused perhaps the greatest amount of public distress with large corporations. Promises of service and customer satisfaction often prove to be hard to fulfill when problems occur with a given product. Consumers become very angry when organizations are not responsive to requests for service or redress. In the 1980s, of course, customer satisfaction has become an obsession with many companies,[14] but many firms still promise far more than they deliver.

Under-the-counter payments. Kickbacks. False representation. Get-rich-quick schemes. These are all symptoms of an ethical crisis in marketing. They play off consumer fear or greed, and they reflect a variety of "manipulation" schemes that characterize a "level one" organization. In the information age, an obsession for customer satisfaction and an orientation to customer benefits will be survival requirements. Forming interdepedent relationships will be necessary for growth.

Exemplars

An example of an ethical exemplar in winning with customers is pharmaceutical giant Johnson & Johnson Inc. (J&J) of New Jersey. On September 30, 1982, James Burke, J&J's CEO, heard that three persons in the Chicago area had died after taking Tylenol capsules. Authorities found that the country's most successful over-the-counter pain reliever had been laced with lethal doses of cyanide.

Tylenol is produced by J&J's McNeil Consumer Products. Its sales were expected to reach $500 million in 1983. In 1981, Tylenol held 37 percent of the $1.5 billion analgesic market, and contributed more than 15 percent to J&J's total earnings of $467 million.[15]

Within days of the first fatality report, the death toll rose to seven—all from the Chicago area. The Tylenol murders were front-page news all over the nation.

As the world well knows, J&J voluntarily initiated a massive recall of 31 million bottles of Extra Strength Tylenol. Burke flew to Washington and met with the commissioner of the FDA and with the FBI Director to jointly work out plans to effect the recall and to make it impossible for the tragedy to stimulate copycat crimes. Burke then called a meeting of 50 J&J company presidents and corporate staffers and made an "unequivocal decision" to put the full resources of J&J behind the recall effort.

At McNeil several teams of employees dealt with the complex problems of resurrecting the Tylenol business and quickly designing tamper-resisitant packaging methods. On November 4, Burke demonstrated a new packaging system in Washington. J&J had devised a triple system of barriers to protect the capsules from tampering. Richard Schweiker, Secretary of Health and Human Services, called the new packaging system an "armored tank."

J&J handled this "distribution problem" correctly. But "doing it right" for J&J in this case was not an isolated event; it was a result of a corporate culture that was driven by ethics and commitment to people.[16] Today, Johnson and Johnson is a healthy and profitable company.

While the Tylenol case represents a dramatic example of the relationship between ethics and profitability, customer relations decisions are made every day that are laced with ethical considerations.

Chemical Bank of New York is another example of an ethical exemplar in the area of winning with customers. Chemical is the fourth largest bank in the United States with approximately $75 billion in assets. It employs more than 30,000 people and is noted for its innovative approach both to business ethics and to corporate responsibility. This foundation is based in the bank's traditional values. There is a pervasive sense of responsibility to others and a sense of fairness toward all stakeholders.

Chemical Bank has been identified as an ethical exemplar for product design because of its uniqe form of outreach to the local community, called "streetbanking." According to the Ethics Resource Center (ERC) in Washington, D.C.:

> "The program was begun in 1969 out of the recognition that banks should be more responsive to the needs of the disadvantaged. Chemical decided to get bankers out into the city's neighborhoods to get to know the local community, its businesses, and its people, and to look for needs and opportunities. Street-bankers are not lending officers, but they look for ways to direct loans, grants, and technical assistance to help small and disadvantaged businesses, aid in the economic development of needy communites, and promote small, grass-roots organizations that may be overlooked by large donors."

Some of the projects that were born out of the street-banking concept include the following:

1971:   created a special lending unit for minority owned, small businesses and became the first bank to hire ex-offenders.

1974:   established an urban housing group designed to rehabilitate low-income housing and create new multiple family dwellings.

1978:   began a program of formal technical assistance to community groups, helping them in such areas as fundraising and financial accounting.

1985:   provided more than $25 million in loans for the rehabilitation of low and moderate income multifamily housing.

Today, Chemical Bank's community efforts include support for social service providers, and programs in housing, literacy, drop-out prevention, teenage pregnancy prevention, and jobs training.

Chemical Bank employs six streetbankers who spend four days a week in their communities getting to know local leaders, businesspeople, and community organizers. Part of the streetbankers' job is to create community profiles, which enable the bank to do a needs assessment and determine the worthiness of various causes. The streetbankers program has an annual budget of $620,000.

The streetbankers program is just one example of the importance of ethics in the Bank's corporate culture. Other examples include the bank's refusal to

- do business with massage parlors or pornographers
- finance arms exports or corporate raiders
- do business with South Africa.

In addition, Chemical Bank has an enviable record in terms of corporate giving and voluntarism. In 1986, Chemical made contributions totaling more than 2 percent of its net earnings after taxes—the U.S. corporate average is 1.2 percent of after-tax income. The bank sponsors a wide variety of cultural, artistic, educational and charitable organizations. Chemical strongly encourages voluntary employee involvement in civic and charitable activities through publicity and an internal

"Volunteer of the Month" program. Chemical's chairman sets an example by serving as chairman of Goodwill Industries.

Two points need to be made here. One, it is unlikely that an isolated program would ever be successful or have much of an impact unless the corporate culture supported activities like it. In this case, the streetbankers program would have been seen as a farce if it had not been congruent with "the ways things work" at Chemical Bank. And two, an ethical culture is easier to maintain when the programs contribute to strategic positioning. For Chemical Bank, the Ethics Resource Center reported in 1988, "poverty, lack of education, and general social decay translate into decreased business opportunities and a higher cost of doing business. ...Thus, Chemical Bank's programs to strengthen its relationship with customers and with the community ultimately benefit the bank."

Challenge

This chapter addresses ethical connections in all phases of the business. The principle focus is on conducting all interactions related to customers with the highest levels of integrity and honesty—from product development through servicing—so that both the company and its customers win.

Several issues related to product development, manufacturing, and marketing are raised. The basic questions that organizations need to ask themselves as an ethical check are:

- Am I trying to manipulate the customer or benefit the customer?

- Are my actions congruent with the strategy of developing interdependent relationships with my customers?

- Do my actions meet the highest standards of integrity and honesty?

- Is my basic marketing strategy a winner?

The challenge to ethical leaders, who are committed to winning with customers, is to cast themselves in a helping role with their clients. Instead of viewing customers as potential consumers of goods and services who can satisfy the providers' financial problems, customers are seen as clients or partners with a wide range of needs for which they need solutions. In this new role, the provider offers integrated solutions to the customer's human, information, organizational and financial problems.[17] In short, the challenge is to move from being self-centered to interdependent.

CHAPTER FOUR

WINNING FOR THE COMMUNITY

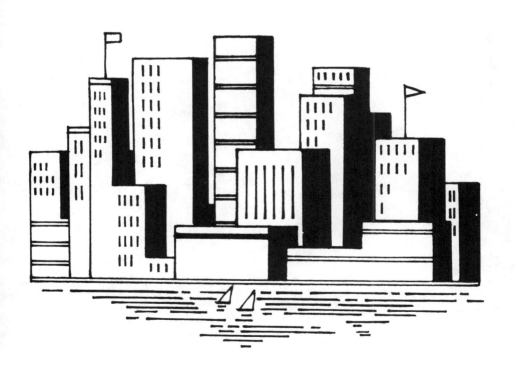

Introduction

What is the mission of an ethical leader?

- Promoting individual and corporate prosperity independent of the long-term effects on the world community?

- Creating a productive and peaceful world community that supports sustainable growth for individuals, groups and organizations?

The answer to this question will determine an organization's readiness to hear this introduction. The following material is blunt in its presentation and frightening in its implications. Content is drawn heavily from the work of the World Commission on Environment and Development which was published in a book, *Our Common Future.* The book's essential premise is that economic growth and environmental hope are inextricably linked. In short, *Our Common Future* suggests that all of our economic policies and business practices need to be considered in terms of sustainable development. This compelling notion looks at ways to meet the needs of the present without compromising the ability of future generations to meet their own needs. It requires meeting the basic needs of all, and extending to all the opportunity to satisfy their aspirations for a better life. This view operationalizes the long term perspective with which business leaders are constantly implored to concern themselves.

Our recent history has not been based on the principles of sustainable development. Quite the contrary—the world is horrified in retrospect as it awakens to its passive acceptance of innumerable atrocities in its brief history. And prospectively, the world still sleeps as its atrocities mount to heights never before imagined. We can't seem to wake up to the genocide we are perpetuating with our passive acceptance of non-sustainable development policies and actions. We can't seem to embrace the idea of sustainable development and use it as a driving force for all our actions.

The authors hope your conclusion from reading the next several pages will be that we can no longer postpone this imperative. Our community, the planet Earth and all the species that inhabit it, demand the immediate attention of ethical leaders.

Witness some examples of what has happened in the last decade.

- An estimated 60 million people died of diarrheal diseases related to unsafe drinking water and malnutrition; most of the victims were children.

- The drought-triggered, environmental crisis in Africa put 35 million people at risk and killed more than 1 million people.

- A leak from a pesticides factory in Bhopal, India killed more than 2,000 people, and more than 200,000 other people were blinded and injured.

- Liquid gas tanks exploded in Mexico City, killing 1,000 people and leaving thousands more homeless.

- The Chernobyl nuclear reactor explosion in the Soviet Union sent nuclear fallout across the world, increasing the risk of future human cancers, particularly in Europe.

- Agricultural chemicals, solvents, and Mercury flowed into the Rhine River during a warehouse fire in Switzerland, killing millions of fish and threatening drinking water in Germany and the Netherlands.[1]

As alarming as these facts are, they may be over-shadowed by future disasters if dramatic changes don't occur immediately. The following review of six key factors in sustainable development makes a compelling case for drastic intervention. The discussion of each factor will include a brief explanation, some facts drawn from work of the World Commission On Environment and Development, and some implications.

1. *Poverty*

Facts

Per capita Gross Domestic Product (GDP) has fallen for developing countries by an average of 10 percent in the 1980s. And world debt increased to $950 billion by 1985—30 percent of which is owed by Argentina, Brazil, Mexico, and Venezuela.[2]

Developed countries account for 26 percent of the population but consume about:

> 40% of the food
> 85% of paper
> 80% of steel
> 80% of energy

The last three items, of course, are as much signs of development as they are symptoms of greed.

In developing countries, 50 percent of the population was below the poverty line in 1985. Income is distributed as follows:

top one-fifth = 50% of total income
bottom four-fifths = 50% of total income[3]

The number of years required to bring the poverty ratio down from 50% to 10% ranges from:

18-24 years at 3% increase/year in per capita GDP
26-36 years at 2% increase/year in per capita GDP
51-70 years at 1% increase/year in per capita GDP[4]

Implications for the ethical leader: There is no sin in creating wealth. In fact, economic productivity growth is essential if we are to have a positive impact on our communities. The question is how the wealth gets distributed. As demonstrated above, it is critical to achieve 3 percent per capita national income growth and to pursue vigorous redistributive policies.

The requirements for such growth include freer market access, lower interest rates, greater technology transfer and larger capital flows. But perhaps, more important, economic productivity growth will require an investment in the human and information resources, which interacting synergistically, will create new responses to challenges that will continue to confront us. In short, jobs and education will generate hope for the future.

2. *Population:* Sustainable development is tied to population and poverty. Poverty reduces people's capacity to use resources in a sustainable manner. And poverty deepens in direct proportion to population growth.

Facts

Between 1985 and 2025, the total population of the industrialized world could increase from its current 1.2 billion to about 1.4 billion, but in developing countries the increase will be from 3.7 billion to 6.8 billion Thus, we can anticipate a world population of 8.2 billion by 2025—a 60 percent increase over roughly three decades.[5]

Between 1985 and 2000 the labor force in developing countries will increase by nearly 900 million people and new jobs will have to be created for 60 million people every year.[6]

By 2000, there will be an additional 900 million people unable to read and write.[7] Education, training and job opportunities will be limited.

Implications for the ethical leader: Unless new jobs are created and poverty abated, the resource base on which sustainable development depends will be further eroded. Thus, the reduction of poverty is a first priority for businesses who are concerned about future growth and long-term development. Otherwise, there is a downward spiral through which people accelerate, resulting in a loss of hope.

3. **_Production:_** In order to meet the demands of a growing population and to fuel a growth economy, goods and services need to be produced. The way the production cycle is handled, from extraction of materials to disposal of wastes, plays a major role in sustainable development.

Facts

We now manufacture seven times the amount of goods we manufactured in 1950. Given expected population growth, an additional five- to tenfold increase in world industrial output can be anticipated by the time we reach the 8 to10 billion population mark.[8] We have witnessed trends toward increased efficiency. The amount of raw materials needed for a given unit of economic output has been dropping throughout this century, except in periods of world war, for practically all non-agricultural commodities. A recent study of consumption trends of seven basic materials in the United States bears this out, as do studies in Japan. Japan used only 60 percent as much raw materials for every unit of industrial production in 1984 as it used in 1973. The productivity and efficiency of resource use are constantly improving, and industrial production is steadily switching away from heavily material-intensive products and processes.[9]

There is clearly a need for regulations. We do need standards to govern such matters as air and water pollution; waste management; occupational health and safety of workers; energy and resource efficiency of products or processes;

and the manufacture, marketing, use, transport and disposal of toxic substances.[10]

With regulation, abuses occur; without regulation, abuses occur with complete abandon. For example, of India's 3,119 towns and cities only 209 have partial sewage and sewage treatment facilities and only eight communities have fully developed sewage facilities. On the river Ganges, 114 cities each with 50,000 or more inhabitants dump untreated sewage into the river every day. Pesticide factories, tanneries, paper and pulp mills, petro-chemical and fertilizer complexes, rubber factories, and a host of other industrial facilities use the river to get rid of their wastes. The Hoogly estuary is choked with untreated industrial wastes from more than 150 major factories around Calcutta. Sixty per cent of Calcutta's population suffer from pneumonia, bronchitis, and other respiratory diseases related to air pollution.[11]

Industries in mainland China, most of which use coal in outdated furnaces and boilers, are concentrated around 20 cities and are responsible for a high level of air pollution. Lung cancer mortality in Chinese cities is four to seven times higher than in the nation as a whole, and the difference is largely attributable to heavy air pollution.[12]

There are 60,000 to 80,000 chemicals now in the market worldwide. There are an average of 56 accidents per day involving chemicals. Industrialized countries generate about 90 percent of the world's hazardous wastes.[13]

Implications for the ethical leader: As the quantity of products and associated wastes continue to increase, at the same time that availability of disposal options continues to decrease, product development and waste disposal issues will climb to the top of priority lists. Business leaders will be required to choose: create environmentally friendly products or fight legislation.

4. *Food and water:* All species need food and water as a source of energy to sustain their own development. Thus, food and water sources for all species need to be protected and enhanced in order to meet the demands of a growing population and the requirement for increased productivity.

Facts

The world produces more food per head today than ever before. It produces nearly 500 kg per head of cereals and root crops, the primary sources of food. Yet, more than 730 million people are not eating enough to lead fully productive working lives.[14]

Sixty-four countries lack the resources to feed themselves. This could be reduced to 19 if advanced agricultural methods were applied.[15]

Potential production capacity could sustain 11 billion people—more than twice the world's current population—assuming current consumption levels. If consumption goes up, the potential capacity would feed 7.5 billion. Experts predict an ultimate world population of 10 billion. Thus, unless we reduce consumption and increase sustainable development, 2.5 billion people will not get sufficient food.[16] This does not account for increasing life expectancy and decreasing infant mortality.

Some governments are taking steps to solve the problem. For example, in the U.S. and in the European Economic Community (EEC), there are massive farm support programs. But these have their own set of economic and environmental costs.

Cost of farm support:

	1980	1986
US	$2.7 billion	$25.8 billion
EEC	$6.2 billion	$21.5 billion[17]

Short-sighted policies are leading to the degradation of the agricultural resource base on almost every continent. The dangerous trends include soil erosion in North America; soil acidification in Europe; and deforestation and desertification almost everywhere. Within 40–70 years, global warming may cause the flooding of important coastal production areas. Some of these effects arise from trends in energy use and industrial resources. But agricultural policies emphasizing increased production at the expense of environmental considerations have also contributed greatly to this deterioration.[18]

While chemical fertilizers and pesticides have played a large role in production increases since the Second World War, clear warnings have been raised against over-reliance on them. The runoff into local water supplies of nitrogen and phosphates from excess use of fertilizers damages water resources, and such damage is spreading. Using chemicals to control insects, pests, weeds, and fungi enhances productivity, but overuse threatens the health of humans and the lives of other species. Continuing, long-term exposure to pesticide and chemical residues in food, water, and even in the air is hazardous, particularly to children. For example, a 1983 study estimated that approximately 10,000 people died each year in developing countries from pesticide poisoning and about 400,000 suffered acutely.[19]

Global water use doubled between 1940 and 1980 and it is expected to double again by 2000, with two-thirds of the projected water use going to agriculture. Yet 80 countries, with 40 percent of the world's population, already suffer serious water shortages.[20]

Some 29 percent of the earth's land area suffers slight, moderate, or severe desertification; an additional 6 percent is classified as extremely desertified. In 1984, the world's drylands supported some 850 million people, of whom 230 million were on lands affected by severe desertification.[21]

The portion of land permanently degraded to desert-like conditions continues to grow at an annual rate of six million hectares. Each year, 21 million additional hectares provide no economic return because of the spread of desertification.[22]

Implications for the ethical leader: The challenge is to meet increased food demands while enhancing ecological integrity. Clearly, starvation anywhere in our community is morally and ethically unacceptable. It is also intolerable for economic and environmental reasons. While food relief programs reduce immediate crises, they lead to further economic marginalization of people over time. People need to be enriched with skills as well as food. Perhaps the goal should be to provide food in a classroom or training facility.

5. *Energy:* Energy requirements are increasing rapidly, while resources are being depleted. It appears that we are moving into a high energy future. Sustainable energy development will require that we find better ways to meet our energy needs.

Here are some basic terms that will facilitate this discussion:

Facts

1 kilowatt	=	1000 watts of energy
1 terawatt (TW)	=	1 billion kilowatts
1 TW year	=	1 billion tons of coal

In 1980, global energy consumption was about 10TW. If per capita use remained at the same levels as today, by 2025 a global population of 8.2 billion would need about 14TW. But if energy consumption per head became uniform worldwide at current industrial country levels, by 2025 that same global population would require about 55 TW.[23]

In 1980, the primary sources of energy were:

coal	4.2 TW
natural gas	2.4 TW
renewables sources	1.7 TW
nuclear	2 TW[24]

At current rates, gas supplies should last over 200 years and coal supplies about 3,000 years. In terms of pollution, gas is the cleanest, oil is the next and coal is the worst.[25]

Renewable energy sources could, in theory, provide 10 to 13 TW annually—equal to current global energy consumption. Today they provide about 2 TW annually, about 21 percent of the energy consumed worldwide, of which 15 percent is biomass and 6 per cent hydropower. However, most of the biomass is in the form of fuel wood and agricultural and animal wastes. As noted above, fuel wood can no longer be thought of as a renewable resource in many areas, because consumption rates have overtaken sustainable yields.[26]

Although worldwide reliance on all these renewable sources has been growing by more than 10 percent per year since the late 1970s, it will be some time before they make up a substantial portion of the world's energy capacity. Renewable energy systems are still in a relatively primitive stage of development. But they offer the world potentially huge primary energy sources, sustainable in perpetuity and available in one form or another to every nation on earth. But it will require a substantial and sustained commitment to further research and development if their potential is to be realized.[27]

Along with these, a major problem arises from the growing scarcity of fuel wood in developing countries. If trends continue, by the year 2000 approximately 2.4 billion people may be living in areas where wood is extremely scarce.[28]

In developing countries, 70 percent of people use wood. Depending on the availability of wood, Third World residents burn anywhere between 350 kg and 2,900 kg of dry wood per person annually, with the average being around 700 kg per person. Rural fuel wood supplies appear to be steadily collapsing in many developing countries, especially in sub-Saharan Africa. At the same time, the rapid growth of agriculture, the pace of migration to cities, and the growing numbers of people entering the money economy are placing unprecedented pressures on the biomass base and increasing the demand for commercial fuels.[29]

Hydropower, second to wood among the renewables, has been expanding at nearly 4 percent annually. Although hundreds of thousands of megawatts of hydropower have been harnessed throughout the world, the remaining potential is huge. In neighboring developing countries, interstate co-operation in hydropower development could revolutionize supply potential, especially in Africa.[30]

Solar energy use is small globally, but it is beginning to assume an important place in the energy consumption patterns of some countries. Solar water and household heating is widespread in many parts of Australia, Greece and the Middle East.[31]

Other renewables include wind power, fuel alcohol, and geothermal energy.[32]

Burning of fossil fuels + loss of vegetation cover = CO_2 pollution. The following chart shows the approximate parts per million of CO_2 in our environment.

1880	280 parts per million
1980	340 parts per million
2100 (estimate)	560 parts per million[33]

At 400 parts per million the result could be a global warming from 1.5 to 4.5 degrees *C*. This development, which would lead to a sea level rise of 25 to140 cm, could inundate low-lying coastal areas. By the year 2025, it is possible that we will reach 400 parts per million.[34]

The U.S. is the principal source of carbon dioxide in the world, producing 23 percent of the total, according to United Nations figures from 1985. The Soviet Union produced 19 percent followed by China with 10 percent, and Japan with 5 percent. In November, 1989, the United States joined with Japan to block agreement by 68 nations to accept strong measures for curbing the release of carbon dioxide into the atmosphere. Both nations said they would not endorse a commitment to control emission of carbon dioxide by the year 2000.

The major sources of carbon dioxide pollution in the U.S. are:

Electric plants	33%
Vehicles	31%
Industries	24%
Other	12%

Implications for the ethical leader: Seeking out renewable, non-polluting sources of energy is a critical issue. Our current energy sources are not only causing enormous pollution problems, they are also impacting the ethical leader who is concerned about long-term energy availability for her or his organizations. These leaders will aggressively scrutinize current energy sources and aggressively seek out practical alternatives.

The economic implications of a high energy future are disturbing. A recent World Bank study indicates that for the period 1980 to 95, a 4.1 percent annual growth in energy consumption would require an average annual investment of some $130 billion in developing countries alone. This would involve doubling the share of energy investment in terms of aggregate gross domestic product.[35]

The environmental risks and uncertainties of a high energy future also give rise to several reservations. These two risks stand out:

- The combustion of fossil fuels contributes to climate changes generated by the greenhouse effect of gases emitted to the atmosphere, most important of which is carbon dioxide (CO). They also cause acidification of the environment and urban industrial air pollution.

- The use of nuclear energy increases the risks associated with dismantling reactors after their service life is over.

But this is not enough. Failures to manage the environment and to sustain development threaten to overwhelm all countries. Environment and development are not separate challenges; they are inexorably linked. Development cannot subsist upon a deteriorating environmental resource base; the environment cannot be protected when growth does not account for the costs of environmental destruction. These problems cannot be treated separately by fragmented institutions and policies. They are linked in a complex system of cause and effect.[36]

As our image of community broadens to the point where we see ourselves as truly global in operations, these factors will play a larger and larger role.

6. *Species Extinction:* Just as our image of community needs to broaden to include the whole world, our notion of life needs to deepen to include all species. Yes, we are feeling embarrassed as human beings with our current practices and narrow passions. And we should. We are, in effect, extinguishing whole families of species.

Facts

If tropical forests continue to be cleared at the current rate, more than 500 million acres will disappear by the year 2000; if destruction of the tropical rain forests continues unabated, an estimated 10 to 20 percent of the earth's plant and animal life will be gone by 2000.[37]

With the destruction of forests, we are rapidly killing various species of plants and animals. Since 1950, in Madasgascar and Western Ecuador, there were over 200,000 species; now fewer than half of these species remain.[38]

Implications for the ethical leader: These are not only ecosystem issues; they are economic issues as well. Wild species contribute to medicine. Half of all prescriptions dispensed have their origins in wild organisms. And sales of these medicines exceed $14 billion per year.[39]

These six factors related to sustainable development—economics, population, production, food and water, energy and species extinction—affect our ability to grow globally. And North America is not exempt from these issues. From 1979 to 1987 the standard of living for the poorest fifth of the population fell below 9 percent. At the same time, the living standard of the top fifth rose by 19 percent. Independent of where one places the blame for this widening gap of income distribution, the shock waves are being felt by communities throughout North America.[40]

This chapter addresses some of the fundamental attitudes and behaviors that would indicate readiness on the part of an organization to get involved in the creation of a productive community. It is the authors' hope that organizations "get ready" soon. The prosperity and freedom of North America are at stake. It cannot be overstated: the future of the world is at risk.

Overview

Vision

Winning for the community means taking the initiative to create productive communities which are able to sustain growth and development.

These are the assumptions related to the connection between sustainable development and economic productivity growth. Companies that treat communities right:

- create the economic base that gives future generations a fighting chance for peace and prosperity.
- improve relationships with local, state, national and international government and civic organizations.
- establish an image in the community as a responsible, responsive and environmentally sensitive contributor.
- demonstrate to employees that the organization has a mission that goes beyond self interest.

Principles

A company that wants to do right by its community will:

1. **Enhance** the environment.
2. **Contribute** generously to community resources.
3. **Encourage** participation in the community.

Rating scale for winning for the community:

Here is a rating scale to help you determine where you are and where you want to be:

5.0	Creating a productive community
4.0	Promoting community growth
3.0	Participating in community organizations
2.0	Protecting community resources
1.0	Polluting

For ratings of specific aspects of this area, please consult Appendix A.

Environment

The Issues

The 1989 communique, agreed to by the major industrial democracies known as the Group of Seven, calls for "decisive action" to protect the global environment. This document places the environment, an afterthought at previous summit meetings, at the top of their agenda for the world economy. While these declarations are more often statements of desire and determination than commitments for change, they often lead to changes in the countries' economic policies. In North America, several companies are also giving the environment a higher place on their internal agendas.

W.S. Woolard, Chairman, E.I. du Pont de Nemours Co., makes this fundamental challenge to companies like Du Pont: "Our continued existence as a leading manufacturer requires that we excel in environmental performance and that we enjoy the non-objection—indeed even the support—of the people and governments in the societies where we operate around the world. What's at stake is the ability of much of our present manufacturing industry to continue to serve well the growing needs of society." Woolard's statement underscores the intimate relationship between environmental ethics and future business success.[42]

Particularly as companies expand into global markets, environmental issues must be addressed. In April 1988, the *Economist* reported that when West Germans were asked what worries them most, twice as many said pollution as said unemployment. In the same month, *Britain's Financial Times* reported that 70 percent of people in the Netherlands said they were prepared to forego a higher standard of living for a cleaner country. Environmental sensitivity is no longer a peripheral issue.[43]

Three Mile Island; Bhopal; Chernobyl; Valdez; the ozone layer: These words are now inscribed in our memory as reminders that disasters can and do occur when we get sloppy.

As a result of these catastrophes and several other environmental warning signs, the public is demanding that organizations take responsible action to protect and enhance our environment. For example:

- North America is quickly moving to a much tighter time frame on CFC's and halons than called for in the 1987 International Montreal Protocol Conference on ozone depletion. The ethical leader will make strong points with worldwide customers by acting aggressively in these areas.

- Agreements with waste transporters, handlers and disposal companies are not uniformly supervised by environmental professionals, nor documented and tracked as defensive data against future litigation and regulatory discipline actions. This leaves organizations vulnerable to guilt by association. The ethical organization will want to know how its waste is being disposed.

- Most companies do not know where all of their underground storage tanks are, what is or was in them, their condition, and whether soil or ground water contamination has or could soon appear. When tanks leak, the costs can be astronomical. For example, one Canadian company just spent $4,700 to clean up a $50 diesel fuel spill. Inadequate monitoring and dismantling of these tanks represents a major liability. In another company, leakage from storage drums has resulted in projected costs in excess of $5 million.[44] Obviously, stringent ethical requirements have economic implications.

- In most companies, there is a lack of planning and resources to ensure that the facilities that companies are currently sitting on will meet the broadest standards of cleanliness. All real estate transactions now require environmental damage assessments, for which companies will continue to have liability. Organizations that act irresponsibly in getting rid of environmental problems may soon be subject to tougher standards. The recent disclosure that toxic waste is being dumped into gas and oil delivery trucks and sold to gas stations where consumers fill their tanks with it demonstrates how pervasive and insidious the problem has become. One reason for this callous disregard of our environment, and of our responsibility to protect it, is the increasing costs of waste disposal. The drums of toxic waste, for example, cost the disposing companies $1,000 per barrel to get rid of.[45] And waste disposal costs are increasing rapidly. This kind of climate is ripe for an unethical entrepreneur to offer discounted prices to collect, transport and dispose of the waste. In this case, the waste was disposed in delivery trucks and distributed to end users at discounted prices. In strictly economic terms, everyone won. The company that created the waste was able to get rid of it at lower rates. The "waste management company" was able to collect substantial fees and avoid the costs of legal disposal. And the consumer was able to purchase "gas" at lower prices because it was laced with chemicals.

One major problem is that most companies have no data management system to ensure compliance, track chemical use and waste production that will meet governmental regulations. Nor are they able to respond to regulatory requests and efficiently manage environmental data. The absence of such systems makes it almost impossible for companies who want to do the right thing to do it. The companies who are determined to take the ethical approach to environmental issues are developing those systems now.

Resources

The Issues

H. Brewster Atwater, the chairman of General Mills Inc. of Minneapolis, has argued that "one of the most important duties of each citizen, whether a corporation or an individual, is to work in a multitude of ways for the betterment of society. In the long run this is a self-interested proposition, in no way inconsistent with a corporation's duties to its shareholders."

Since 1970, corporate philanthropy has grown more than twice as rapidly as that of private foundations. Corporations in the U.S donated an estimated $3.45 billion in 1984, approaching the $4.36 billion given by foundations. As part of the effort by the Ronald Reagan administration to increase corporate social giving and "public-private" partnerships," its Task Force on Private Sector Initiatives set a goal in 1981 of increasing corporate giving from an average 1 percent of pre-tax net earnings to 2 percent by 1986. Figures reported by the American Association of Fund-Raising Councils show the corporate average hovering around 1.5 percent from 1982 through 1984.[46]

The California Chamber of Commerce has been promoting the formation of "Two-Percent Clubs" around the state since 1983. Minneapolis's Dayton Hudson Corporation is a strong advocate of "five-percent" giving levels.

There is, of course, an endless array of organizations and causes that solicit corporate funds. Most organizations, however, concentrate their giving in a few key areas. The following chart shows the areas in which corporations allocated their charitable contributions.

Education	40%
Health and human services	30%
Civic and community	15%
Culture and art	10%
Other	5%[22]

Productive Communities

The Issues

Madelyn Jennings, senior vice-president for personnel at Gannett Co., the Arlington, Virginia-based newspaper chain that publishes USA Today, says, "We are looking a lot harder in places that we haven't focused our attention on: the disabled, retired, older workers. It has nothing to do with altruism or concern about society. It has to do with survival. We are going to have to get more and more involved in the issues of drug abuse, productivity, accidents, managing health care costs and the education system. These are social issues, but they are very much at the heart of a company doing well."[47]

And according to Theodore Payne, manager of corporate affirmative action at Xerox Corporation of Stamford, Conn., "We get no help from any other institution in America. The country is deficient in education and deficient in social and moral values. We have to do it ourselves. Sometimes I am disheartened, but we have to do it—we have no choice."[48]

These remarks demonstrate the connection between social responsibility and corporate needs. Currently, many organizations are assuming that communities will provide the human resources required to maintain a steady stream of people and ideas. This assumption, which relates to the lifeblood of the future, needs to be challenged. If companies are counting on continual revitalization in the future, they will need to revitalize the communities on whom they depend.

Communities consist of homes, schools, universities, businesses, and arts/leisure facilities and organizations. They are effected by political, social, economic and environmental factors. While businesses cannot be expected to solve all the problems of the communities in which they reside, they will need to establish interdependent relationships with all the entities so that collaborative initiatives can be launched.

Exemplars

An example of an ethics exemplar in the area of winning for communites is du Pont, headquartered in Wilmington, Delaware. The firm is the largest chemical company in the U.S. with annual sales of $32.5 billion. du Pont has developed a corporate agenda for environmental leadership for the next decade. Here are some of the goals that the chairman of duPont expects to accomplish by the year 2000 or before:

- du Pont manufacturing facilities have had a goal of 35 percent reduction at the source of total hazardous waste by 1990. du Pont will at least duplicate that level of progress during the next decade. Waste reduction will be one of du Pont's primary technical objectives during the 1990s.

- du Pont will eliminate heavy metal pigments used in the manufacture of some plastics.

- du Pont will take an increasing responsibility for the efficient and environmentally acceptable disposal of the plastic portion of the global solid waste stream.

- du Pont will extend the practice of including community representatives in discussions of present and planned local plant operations.

- du Pont will consider environmental performance in a direct and formal way—both pro and con—in determining compensation from middle management to senior officers of the company.[49]

Behind all these commitments is du Pont's objective to become one of the world's most environmentally sound manufacturing companies and to make sure that the world knows it. It appears that du Pont is making excellent progress on that goal. In 1988, in a *Fortune* magazine survey, the chief executives of top U.S. companies ranked du Pont second in terms of overall environmental performance and first among chemical companies.

GTE Corp. of Stamford, Conn., a major telecommunications company, is another example of an ethics exemplar in the area of winning for the community. GTE's Volunteer Initiatives Program helps match employee volunteers with local organizations, and provides additional grants of up to $1,000 to those organizations. GTE estimates it gave out a substantial $500,000 in VIP grants in 1985.[50]

More and more companies are attempting to become exemplars in the area of developing community resources. Eastman Kodak Co., while it is a big polluter, is helping restructure the school system in Rochester, N.Y., where the firm is headquartered. General Electric Co. is working on programs to get more minority teachers into colleges and universities. Sears Roebuck & Co. together with 14 other firms, has funded a model school that works with inner-city students. Aetna Life and Casualty Co., based in Hartford, Conn. is working with local organizations to teach reading and writing to 19- to 24-year-olds. These are just a few examples of companies who not only recognize the problems inherent in the erosion of community resources and marketable skills, but also are taking bold initiatives to contribute to the solution.

At first glance, McDonald's restaurants could be targeted as a company in need of ethical change. After all, it is one of the largest purveyors of high-sodium, high-fat, fast foods in North America and its packaging contributes to the litter problems in our communities. The authors admit to being guilty of assuming the worst about McDonald's because of its product line. In fact, we wrote a letter to the President of McDonald's suggesting a three-phase campaign to change their image: McFit, a vegetarian sandwich; McSafe, an incentive program to encourage seat belt use; and McLitter, an initiative to clean up debris in the community. The response from McDonald's Canada and our subsequent investigation, however, revealed some surprising findings about McDonald's efforts, particularly in Canada, to become an ethics exemplar. Here is a summary of what we found.

In order to respond to growing awareness of healthy lifestyles and diets, McDonald's changed its menu to be more customer oriented. Some examples include the introduction of salads in 1988, the reduction of the sodium content in cheese, pickles and sausage; the addition of calcium to the buns; the transition from whole milk to 2% milk; and the use of lean beef in the burgers.

In 1984, McDonald's pioneered a major family safety program: Make it Click. This safety seat belt program, which was designed and endorsed by police chiefs throughout Canada, stressed the importance of using seat belts when driving. This children's program ran for three years and was supported by several million pieces of literature, as well as a media campaign to encourage the participation of children and families across the country. In addition to McClick, McDonald's has sponsored bicycle safety programs, Halloween safety programs, and anti-substance abuse videos.

McDonald's is also active in the community. In the first half of 1989, in excess of $600,000 was committed to 19 organizations and three Ronald McDonald Houses. And McDonald's one-day fundraising events raise much-needed funds for Canada's community-based non-profit organizations. The past seven McHappy Days have raised more than $5 million for Canadian children with special needs.

Moreover, McDonald's Canada has an active program for hiring and training handicapped persons.

According to Hal Gregory, Vice President and National Director of Purchasing for McDonald's, "Playing an integral role in the community's well-being is the way McDonald's does business."

McDonald's is also active in environmental issues. It works with suppliers and experts in the industry to explore new packaging, recycling and landfill technologies. McDonald's is working with its suppliers and raw product manufacturers in pilot recycling programs across North America to find practical and effective solutions that will benefit the restaurant industry as well as others. McDonald's also took the industry lead when it instructed suppliers to remove CFC-12 in the manufacture of polystyrene packaging. This step influenced the entire foam packaging industry. As a result, McDonald's was cited at Toronto's recent international environment summit, "Our World," by the environment group, Friends of the Earth, as one example of a few companies who took a lead in the CFC issue.

Recent interest in the world's tropical rain forests and the causes of their destruction, including cattle ranching, sparked growing public concern and inquiries regarding McDonald's sources of beef. McDonald's policy is that it does not and will never use rain forest beef. Again, quoting Hal Gregory, "If there is a better, more environmentally sound way to operate, we will find it and we will do it."

The inclusion of du Pont and McDonald's as exemplars of winning for communities may raise questions. du Pont is known as the developer and producer of napalm and as the largest producer of CFCs in the world. McDonald's, as stated earlier, is associated with high-fat foods and litter. One might ask, are these companies' apparent interest in the community and the environment just a clever public relations scheme to defuse negative public sentiment? Or are these efforts for real? Also, one might ask, is it possible for a company to strive for a high level of ethics when the products it manufactures are inherently destructive? Or is the only ethical solution to end the production of "bad products?"

Perhaps the best way to address these questions is to return to the preface of the book where we first elaborated on this generic issue. From the authors' point of view, the ethical position for du Pont would be to discontinue immediately its production of napalm, CFCs and any other products that are so clearly destructive. In the case of McDonald's, we applaud their efforts to offer healthy alternatives to contribute constructively to the community, and to be environmentally responsible. On the other hand, they have plenty of room for improvement with products like Chicken McNuggets, the Big Mac and Fries. And they should ensure that their advertising campaigns don't suggest that their whole product line is nutritionally sound. It simply is not.

The point is that all of the exemplars cited in this book probably have warts and moles if we look hard enough. The real issue is the genuineness with which these firms are engaging in ethical issues. What is the authenticity with which these firms are approaching their ethical challenges? It is the authors' opinion that the exemplars cited in this book are making genuine efforts to continually improve their ethical commitment.

Challenge

This chapter encourages leaders to explore the readiness factors in their organizations to create more productive communities. Three fundamental indicators suggest the extent to which an organization is truly commited to making a difference: environmental responsibility, charitable giving, and community involvement.

For organizations that have demonstrated a commitment to change, the challenge is to create the capacity for change in resident communities. Homes need to become preparatory learning centers; schools need to become thinking centers; universities need to become creativity centers; and businesses need to become productivity centers.[51] This will not and cannot happen with a wish and a prayer. It will require a substantive, systematic and comprehensive intervention which involves all members of the community. It can be done. It must be done.

CHAPTER FIVE

ACTION STEPS

The first and most important step is to be able to recognize an ethical corporate culture when you see one. Most executives see ethics through a set of "compliance-colored" glasses, however, which limit their view of what an ethical culture might look like. Instead of constantly searching for new possibilities in the ethics-strategy connection, the mind-set tends to be: "Our ethics program is working if there are no fines and no allegations of malfeasance." With "compliance" glasses and an "avoidance" mind-set, it is unlikely that executives will be able to recognize the potential for competitive advantage inherent with high levels of ethics. There must be an emphasis on positive direction.

In a review of more than 100 companies that were considered as ethical exemplars for various sections of this book, we found ten common ingredients that seem to provide a competitive advantage for highly ethical corporate cultures. The action steps translate these ingredients into principles, objectives and programs that will be useful to executives who want to renew the focus on ethics in their organizations or transform their organizations from unacceptable ethics (levels 1.0 or 2.0) to acceptable ethics (level 3.0) or advantageous ethics (levels 4.0 or 5.0). Please refer to Appendix A for specific rating scales on all the issues covered in this book. The following ingredients will help you recognize an ethical culture when you see one.

The ingredients of an ethical culture

1. A tradition of strong values and ethics.
2. A belief at the top in the strategic importance of integrity.
3. Leadership modelling and commitment.
4. Explicit statements of values and beliefs, such as codes of ethics, and standards of business conduct.
5. Active solicitation of support from managers and employees.
6. A common view that ethics is a cultural issue.
7. Procedures and systems which ensure that ethics is a central part of selection and performance management.
8. Tailored education and training programs.
9. Multiple upward and downward communications channels.
10. Broad monitoring of ethics goals.

This chapter contains three sections: Principles and Action Steps which are built around the ten ingredients listed above; an Evaluation Tool which summarizes all of the topic areas covered in this book; and Strategies for Accountability, which will help to reinforce the principles and goals that are selected.

Principles and Action Steps

1. When ethics and values are grounded in tradition, policies emerge naturally as an outgrowth of the culture.

In almost all of the organizations cited as ethical exemplars in this book, major decisions in troubling times were eased by a well-defined set of values that served as anchors in gray and turbulent seas. Thus, the first step for the ethical executive should be to review the values that guide the organization, and assess how accurately those values reflect how things "really work around here." It takes time and energy to develop such a tradition.

2. When integrity is viewed as having strategic importance, all employees begin to see the business possibilities in creating an ethical edge.

Ethical exemplars encourage leaders in their organizations to ask hard questions about issues in every phase of the business. As such, people must feel free to disagree, probe, poke fun and challenge directions or decisions which the company may be facing. One chairman suggested that executive committees should contain a jester, an ethicist and an empiricist. The jester pokes fun at various initiatives, the ethicist raises questions of integrity, and the empiricist seeks out the facts and numbers that make for useful debate. Thus, the second step is to ensure that all employees see the potential of sharpening the ethical edge, and to create an environment that encourages people to think about and debate ethical issues as they arise or, better, to identify them before they spark a crisis.

3. When leadership demonstrates its commitment to ethics through its own behavior, employees will get the message that taking the high road will enhance their careers.

Since employees take their cues from their leaders, executive behavior has a far greater impact on employee ethics than any words, memos or documents distributed from the executive suite. Even relatively innocous indications such as participation in "Decision Making and Corporate Values" seminars similar to what Chemical Bank provides, let employees know that ethics is taken seriously. And leaders benefit from this sort of participation because they have opportunities to share their thinking on case studies and receive feedback on their actions, thoughts and feelings. Thus, the third step is to encourage the leadership team to demonstrate its commitment to creating an ethical edge in a variety of ways.

4. When there are explicit statements of values and beliefs, employees are clear about expectations.

Clarity is essential in the definitions of desired behaviors and corporate culture. In most companies, values are vague notions or undefined lists that are supposed to guide decision making. Thus, the fourth step is to articulate the vision and values of the company, distribute code of conduct books for all employees, write standards of business conduct for all departments, and breathe life into all these documents through ongoing communications and discussions.

5. When executives actively solicit the involvement and support of managers and employees, there is joint ownership of the mission.

All employees need to be encouraged to take the initiative with regard to ethics issues. Open door policies and whistleblowing (if required) should be supported. To bolster enthusiasm for this sort of ethics partnership, a compelling business case goes a long way to persuade management that ethics is a first-priority business need. Involvement and ownership require that programs are personalized for people in various departments. Thus, the fifth step is to announce an ethics partnership program that involves employees at all levels in the process of sharpening the ethical edge.

6. When ethics is seen as a cultural issue, people focus on the environment as a potential source of competitive advantage.

It is a mistake to see ethics as a crusade to rout out evil in the organization. And yet, in many organizations, ethics comes under the purview of narrowly focused security departments buried in the bowels of the human resource department and driven by a mission to catch the bad guys in their organizations. These types are easily recognized by the handcuff tie clips they proudly display. More accurately, in the level 1.0 and 2.0 firms, ethics is purely an accounting function, handled by the internal audit and the corporate secretary or legal affairs persons. In the more progressive firms, ethics may become an HR function. In level 4.0 and 5.0 firms, the CEO directs the ethics program and implementation is every executive's job, regardless of division. "Ethics management" in the level 5.0 firm, becomes a line function versus purely a staff function. Some ethical exemplars may even have trained ethicists in the board rooms helping to guide the organization into the future. Thus, the sixth step is to create a set of norms that influence ethical behavior. This can be initiated by appointing an ethics advisor or an ethics ombudsman who reports to the CEO or to the board. And the company should make an annual practice of conducting an "ethics audit". A note of caution is in order here. Simply making an appointment won't change the culture. The key is CEO ownership of the issue and follow up with everyone in the ranks through training, codes, and recognition of ethical behavior in the reward systems. For example, at Donitar, a performance bonus is determined in part on the basis of an employee's ability to eliminate time lost due to accidents. At Gannett, bonuses are tied in part to success in meeting goals for hiring women and minorities.

7. When values and ethics are central to selection, training and performance management, congruence is approached between what the organization says it's about and values people really hold.

It's a tired maxim, but it's true: people do what they are rewarded for. However, as organizational and personal values become more closely aligned, the rewards evolve synergistically. The organization is rewarded by the commitment the person has to the organization and the person is rewarded by the trust and value the organization places in him or her. This congruence does not just occur accidentally. The organization needs constant infusions from new people, enhanced training programs and rewards and recognition processes. Key positions must be filled from without *and* from within. Irving Trust Co. only promoted from within and became a dead organization. It was eventually taken over by the Bank of New York.

These infusions are constructive to the extent that they reinforce the importance of values in all business transactions. The best way to create an ethical culture is to recruit and retain people who reflect the values and principles of the corporate culture. And conversely, it may be necessary to impose immediate and strict discipline for ethical offenses (behaviors that are inconsistent with organizational values) by those employees who don't represent the desired values and norms. Thus, the seventh step is to review the selection, training and performance management systems to ensure that adequate attention is given and sound measures are available to tighten the fit between organizational and personal values.

8. When education and training programs are tailored to the needs of the target population, people are able to apply the skills in creative and productive ways.

A training program conducted independently of the other nine steps discussed here would be an exercise in futility. However, if it is a central part of a well-orchestrated process to achieve an ethical edge, then education and training serve a critical purpose. Ideally, ethics should be seen as a functional application of productive thinking and relating.[1,2,3] Traditionally, new-employee orientation, management seminars, and decision making courses address the issues of ethics, but most of this training is geared toward compliance issues. Thus, the eighth step is to determine what level of ethics the education and training programs are designed to achieve and decide if that intervention is consistent with your goals. Ultimately, the education and training efforts should produce thinking managers who relate constructively.

9. When there are multiple upward and downward communication channels, employees feel informed about what's going on and free to intitiate their ideas for improvement.

Multiple communication vehicles and channels give employees confidence that ethics issues can be addressed. Employees need to believe there are people in the organization who will hear their ideas for creating an ethical edge. To facilitate upward communications, as mentioned earlier, some companies have created ethics advisors and ombudsman whose job it is to be responsive to employee ideas, suggestions and concerns. In most organizations, there are a variety of vehicles for downward communication, but one effective ethics strategy is to roll out the training from the top, using managers as trainers. This strategy reinforces the importance of ethics, provides the opportunity to integrate ethics into business operations, and enables managers to personalize key principles to their respective units. Thus, the ninth step is to explore options for expanding upward and downward communication. Ethics can't merely be imposed from on high; leaders have to find out from the troops exactly what is going on "down there".

10. When progress toward ethical goals is closely monitored, sustained action is more likely to occur.

Broad monitoring of ethics goals enables executives to establish baseline data, observe trends over time, and set appropriate goals. An Evaluation Tool for

Human and Information Capital Support (ETHICS) is included in Table 3 as an example of a rating system for a comprehensive assessment of ethical possibilities. Specific rating scales are available in Appendix A to derive a "score" for each area. These instruments should be used by an internal audit committee or external consultant to monitor progress on a regular basis. Thus, step 10 is to decide how to monitor progress on your initiatives so that you can sustain your ethical edge.

Strategies for Accountability

Aside from these 10 principles, ethical leadership can be viewed from the perspective of accountability. Using this theme, a number of strategies have been articulated by Fred Bird, a professor of religion at Montreal's Concordia University and a leading authority on business ethics.

1. **Legal accountability.** Legislation is becoming more prolific and severe. Governments around the globe are enacting and enforcing more and more laws related to the way businesses deal with people, customers, and their communities. Particularly in the area of environment, new regulations demand increasing sensitivity to the concept of sustainable development. Essentially, ethical leaders need to make a choice. Do they spend exhorbitant amounts of money trying to lower compliance thresholds by lobbying government bodies to relax legislation? Do they invest in measures that ensure that their organizations go beyond compliance? Or do they try to create

an ethical edge by taking a leadership position in ethics? GM took the "first road." It spent $1.8 billion dollars in the last decade lobbying against enhanced clean air legislation. However, this book contains several examples of companies which have profited by taking the 'high road'.

2. *Market accountability*. Investors, purchasers and job applicants are expanding the list of values and criteria on which they make buying decisions. Business ethics appear regularly on those lists. And "Ethics Monitors" are making information more available on companies' standard business practices. Leaders will need to know how their companies stack up against the competition on ethical criteria as well as product quality. Just as quality was the driving force of the 1980s, ethics could be the driving force of the 1990s and beyond. Organizations such as the New York-based Council for Economic Priorities and the Toronto-based EthicScan are likely to heighten scrutiny and pressure in the 1990s.

3. *Union accountability.* Unions, over the years, have helped to redefine, and thus enhance, ethical practices in business. Unions continue to exert pressure on companies regarding fair employee treatment and safe working conditions. Historically, unions have had a narrow focus at the bargaining table. Their traditional targets are fair wages, safe working conditions, and health and pension benefits. If unions decide to expand their scope to include issues related to the corporate culture, customer relationships, and com-

munity responsibility, they may regain the strength they have lost in recent years. The question is who will seize the initiative to capture the hearts and minds of the people.

4. ***Special interest and professional association accountability.*** People have loyalties that go beyond their organization. Most employees belong to at least one special interest or professional association (such as engineering, medicine or marketing association) or special interest group (such as Ducks Unlimited, church denominations, Greenpeace, the Lung Association or Amnesty International) which have defined sets of values. These values exert a powerful influence on behavior. When corporate values run counter to the values of the other organizations to which employees belong, people will act in accordance with the organizational values with which they are most personally identified.

5. ***Board of director accountability.*** Boards of directors increasingly perceive themselves as "moral assessors". One part of their role is to ensure ethical conduct of the businesses they direct or advise. As this change in the perceived role changes, senior management will get a new message: Movement up and ethical conduct are intimately tied. And standards of ethical conduct will be applied to the aspiring executive's influence on the culture, people, customers and communities with which the organization leads.

6. ***Policy accountability.*** The ethical leader does more than spew out policies and procedures.

She or he not only writes and says the right words, but does the right things. Policies should include statements about what kind of culture the organization wants to create, how it wants to treat its employees and its customers, and how it wants to relate to the community. These policies need to be audited and measured with tools similar to the scales provided throughout this book and in the appendices. Codes of ethics, standards of business conduct, and corporate communications need to be reinforced with sign-offs on understanding and rewards for ethical action.

7. ***Stakeholder accountability.*** You can't rely exclusively on directives coming down from on high. You need to encourage people to speak up. Ethical leaders encourage people to express their concerns; and they don't hold candor against them. They create a culture of openness. And they institute several mechanisms to facilitate an upward flow of information. Ethical leaders not only set the tone, they listen to the pulse. And they serve as resources to their people. Accountability requires open communications, in which people see themselves as stakeholders in the business.

These principles, action steps, and strategies can be simplified by following the brief, implementation outline below:

1. Get a general sense of where you are by studying the scales provided in the overview sections of chapters one through four.

2. Decide where you want to be as an organization.

3. Use the scales in Appendix A to assess where you are in each of the specific topic areas. Fill in the chart provided on the next page.

4. For those areas in which you rated yourself less than 3.0, review the sections in each chapter to develop specific plans in each of those areas to get to level 3.0.

5. For those areas in which you rated yourself 3.0 or more, review the sections in each chapter which discuss the "possibilities" realized by ethics exemplars. Decide what your organization could do to match or exceed the outcomes achieved by these exemplars.

6. Put these questions on the agenda of your staff meeting on a regular basis:

   • How can we create a more ethical culture within our organization?

   • What are the current obstacles or problems in our way?

   • What possiblities may open up for us if we develop an ethical edge?

7. Plan a comprehensive and systematic effort to actualize your ethical vision.

Table 3
AN ETHICS ASSESSMENT AND GOAL SETTING TOOL

Evaluation Tool for Human and Information Capital Support (ETHICS)

CULTURE: 1 2 3 4 5
- — Creating a vision
- — Defining values
- — Embedding norms

PEOPLE
- — Developing employees
- — Promoting health and safety
- — Supporting balance
- — Valuing differences

CUSTOMERS
- — Connecting ethics with product development
- — Connecting ethics with manufacturing
- — Connecting ethics with marketing

COMMUNITIES
- — Enhancing the environment
- — Contributing to community resources
- — Participating in community organizations

SUMMARY

At this point you may be saying, "Well, it all sounds good, but:

- is this just another bandwagon?
- is this going to result in a mass confessional?
- is this going to cost more than it's worth?
- are resources available?"

Ethics is not another bandwagon. Ethical leadership has one outcome: sustainable development. We cannot sustain progress if our corporate culture does not support our policies. We cannot sustain growth if we don't invest in our people and treat them as whole persons with unique gifts. We cannot sustain profits if we don't help our customers achieve their productivity and profitability goals. We cannot sustain development on a global basis if we don't treat the environment more respectfully and assist in the transformation of developing countries into healthier, productive and more prosporous communities.

Ethical leadership does not mean mass confessions or finding a guiding light, or forming a new business religion. Quite the contrary. Ethical leadership is not interested in lies. It seeks the truth. Ethical leadership is not interested in myths. It demands realities. Ethical leadership is hot hardheaded. It is soft-hearted, but tough-minded.

Winning the right way may be expensive. For example, conservation and recycling investments may require substantial outlays in the early stages. Educating people also costs money. Insisting on product safety and customer benefits requires further expenses. However, the cost of trying to win without extraordinary scrutiny to ethics can be disastrous. The cases of Union Carbide's complicity in the Bhopal tragedy and Johns-Manville's slow decline into bankruptcy over product liability lawsuits arising from health problems caused by asbestos illustrate the consequences of ethical sloppiness. And as we saw in Chapter 4, Winning for the Community, the costs of delaying interventions outweigh the costs of immediate initiatives.

It is very difficult to quantify damage-control costs, not least because cost figures are highly dependent on the control strategy assumed. However, in the eastern United States, it has been estimated that halving the remaining sulphur dioxide emissions from existing sources would cost $5 billion per year, increasing electricity rates by 2 to 3 percent. Materials corrosion damage due to CO_2 emissions, however, is estimated to cost $7 billion annually in 17 states in the U.S.[1]

Thousands of waste disposal sites exist, many of which are likely to require some form of remedial action. Cleanup is expensive. Estimates range from $10 billion for West Germany to $100 billion for the United States. However, the health risks of continued contamination far exceeds the amounts quoted here.[2]

Commiting funds to cleanup of past abuses and to prevent future disasters will require a re-distribution of resources. In government, for instance, there will be a requirement to shift allocation of funds from perhaps the military to the environment. President Dwight Eisenhower observed at the end of his term in office that "every gun that is made, every warship launched, every rocket fired represents in the final analysis, a theft from those who hunger and are not fed, who are cold and are not clothed."[3]

The world spent more than $900 billion on military goods and services in 1985, or more than $2.5 billion a day. The real cost is what the same resources might otherwise be used for. For example:

- An action plan for tropical forests would cost an estimated $1.3 billion per year.

- A United Nation's action plan for reversing the desertification process would cost $4.5 billion a year.

- The UN Water and Sanitation Decade, designed to provide clean water for household use in the Third World, would cost $30 billion per year.

- The supply of contraceptive materials to all women already motivated to use family plan-ning would cost $1 billion per year.[4]

Ethical leaders need not feel lonely. There are people throughout the world working on these issues. Here are some recommended sources:

United States:

Ethics Resource Center
1025 Connecticut Ave., N.W.
Suite 1003
Washington, D.C. 20036
202-223-3411

Interfaith Center on Corporate Responsibility
475 Riverside Drive #566

New York, N.Y. 10115
212-870-2936

Council on Economic Priorities
30 Irving Place
New York, N.Y. 10003
212-420-1133

Canada:

Canadian Center for Ethics and Corporate Policy
George Brown House, 2nd floor
50 Baldwin St. at Beverly
Toronto, Ontario M5T1L4
416-348-8691

EthicScan Canada, Ltd. and the Canadian
Clearinghouse for Consumer and Corporate
Ethics
P.O. Box 165, Postal Station 'S'
Toronto, Ontario M5M 4L7
416-783-6776

APPENDIX A

RATING SCALES FOR EACH AREA

CHAPTER ONE: CREATING AN ETHICAL CULTURE

Vision

5.0 SEE THE WORLD AS YOUR COMMUNITY

4.0 SEE THE NATION AS YOUR COMMUNITY

3.0 SEE YOUR CUSTOMERS AS YOUR COMMUNITY

2.0 SEE YOUR EMPLOYEE POPULATION AS PART OF YOUR COMMUNITY

1.O SEE THE COMPANY

At level 1.0, the company does not see itself connected to any community. It sees potential for gain or loss entirely in individualistic management and/or stockholder terms.

At level 2.0, the organization sees the employees as part of their community, but it also sees potential for gain or loss only inwardly.

At level 3.0, the organization sees the customer as an important part of its community. It sees potential for interdependent gain or loss.

At level 4.0, the organization sees the "location" also as its community. It understands the "civic" responsibility of corporations.

At level 5.0, the organization sees the world as its community. And it sees potential for gain or loss in terms of the world community. Level 5.0 organizations strive to achieve full interdependence; believe in open sharing of information; believe in universal connectivity; and work on sustainable development projects.

Values

5.0   ALL MAJOR DECISIONS EVALUATED ON VALUES

4.0   VALUES COMMUNICATED AND MODELLED

3.0   WELL-DEFINED SET OF VALUES

2.0   LOOSELY DEFINED SET OF VALUES

1.0   UNDEFINED VALUES

At level 1.0, the organization has no values that define it in any way. It is totally opportunistic.

At level 2.0, the organization would say it has a set of values, but everyone would define them differently. Activities are independent of value.

At level 3.0, the organization has a well-defined set of values. These values are probably published and framed and may even show up in the annual reports. People at lower levels in the organization, however, don't hear about them or see them practiced.

At level 4.0, the organization communicates its values and models them. People understand what the organization is about.

At level 5.0, all major decisions are evaluated on values. The values are weighted and considered as a whole. There is great resistance in the organization to making single-value decisions.

Norms

5.0 CULTURE REWARDS ETHICAL BUSINESS
PRACTICES

4.0 CULTURE ENCOURAGES ETHICAL BUSINESS
PRACTICES

3.0 CULTURE SUPPORTS ETHICAL BUSINESS
PRACTICES

2.0 CULTURE ACCEPTS UNETHICAL BUSINESS
PRACTICES

1.0 CULTURE ENCOURAGES UNETHICAL
BUSINESS PRACTICES

At level 1.0, the organization encourages unethical business practices. The Robber Baron mentality characterizes these types of organizations.

At level 2.0, the organization accepts unethical practices. If people are caught stealing or engaging in fraud, the offences are often overlooked.

At level 3.0, the organization supports ethical practices. People would say, "around here, people try to win the right way."

At level 4.0, the organization encourages ethical practices. For example, employees who want to participate in community activities are given the time to do so.

At level 5.0, the organization rewards ethical practices. For example, promotions are based, in part, on the way employees treat people, customers and the community.

CHAPTER TWO:
WINNING THROUGH PEOPLE

Employee Development

5.0 INCREASE STREET VALUE
4.0 FUNCTIONAL APPLICATIONS
3.0 GENERIC SKILLS
2.0 CONCEPTS (PROGRAMS WITHOUT SKILLS)
1.0 FACTS

At level 1.0, employees are given only the facts they need to know to do their jobs.

At level 2.0, employees are offered programs which give them a conceptual overview of their job, its function, the skills required to perform the job and how those skills contribute to the organization.

At level 3.0, employees are equipped with an educational core set of skills designed to help them think better, relate more constructively and plan systematically. These skills empower employees to contribute to the organization.

At level 4.0, the generic skills are reinforced with opportunities to learn and practice functional applications (for example: coaching, delegating and conducting performance reviews).

At level 5.0, the organization trains its employees so that their street value meets or exceeds their compensation in their current job. By so doing, the organization reduces employees' fears about instability, insecurity and reductions in force because the employees know they can leave whenever the gap between their personal values and their job requirements is too large. What employees may lose in job security, they will gain in career security. And, at the same time, this type of psychological contract eliminates the pressure on employers to make lifetime employment guarantees. At level 5.0, the ethical organization is freed to achieve a realistic balance between satisfying worker values and meeting stakeholder recommendations. Both the organization and the individual win through improved education.

Health and Safety

5.0   CULTURE CHANGE
4.0   PERSONAL DEVELOPMENT
3.0   PHYSICAL RISK REDUCTION
2.0   FIRST AID, PRIMARY CARE
1.0   FULL RESPONSIBILITY ON EMPLOYEE

At level 1.0, the organization puts full responsibility for health and safety on the employee. There is no attempt to distribute the responsibility appropriately and take commensurate action with that distribution.

At level 2.0, the organization provides first aid and basic primary care. The idea here is to treat workplace injuries on site to increase speed of response, provide convenient service and reduce the time employees are off the job obtaining medical assistance.

At level 3.0, the organization sponsors an array of accident prevention and physical risk reduction programs such as smoking cessation, high blood pressure control, cholesterol reduction, stress management and weight control. These programs are aimed at preventing loss due to sickness or absence.

At level 4.0, the organization supports personal development through a variety of interventions designed to help employees improve their physical, emotional and intellectual well-being. For example, these programs may include fitness, nutrition, interpersonal communication, self-esteem, managing change and creative thinking.

At level 5.0, the organization's focus is to create an environment that supports positive safety and health practices. The emphasis is on culture change and building health partnerships between the individual and the organization. At level 5.0, both the organization and the individual win. The organization gains through a more energetic, enthusiastic and creative work force. And the individual benefits through improved health, vitality and career fulfillment.

Supporting Balance

5.0   ON-SITE DAY CARE AND A FULL RANGE OF FAMILY CARE BENEFITS

4.0   SUBSIDIZED DAY CARE AND SELECTED FAMILY CARE BENEFITS

3.0   COMPUTERIZED REFERRAL SERVICE FOR FAMILY CARE

2.0   RECOGNITION OF CHANGING NEEDS

1.0   DEMAND TRADITIONAL ROLES AND/OR IGNORE CHANGING TRENDS

At level 1.0, organizations demand traditional roles and/or ignore changing trends. In these organizations, there are different expectations for women than for men and there is great resistance to any efforts to support changing roles. Also, these organizations typically leave little room for family needs and are not supportive when issues arise in families from birth or adoption through to illness or death.

At level 2.0, organizations recognize the changing needs of the work force and changing roles of men and women. In these organizations, policies usually reflect some sensitivity to parenting and elder care issues, and allow for generous leaves of absence for issues as they arise.

At level 3.0, organizations have some support services available in the form of computerized referral or personal counselling for employees to find assistance for family related issues.

At level 4.0, organizations provide subsidies for child care and offer selected benefits related to family issues. These organizations encourage people to pursue personal interests.

At level 5.0, the organization is sensitive and responsive to a full range of family and personal needs. On-site day care is provided, leaves of absense are granted for family and personal issues, and elder care needs are understood and supported. Overall, the corporate culture encourages a healthy balance between family and career and treats employees as whole persons.

Valuing Differences

5.0 MEANINGFUL BOARD AND SENIOR MANAGE-
MENT REPRESENTATION OF MINORITIES
AND WOMEN (INCLUSIVITY)

4.0 AGGRESSIVE SUPPORT FOR INTERNAL
PROMOTIONS OF WOMEN AND MINORITIES

3.0 AFFIRMATIVE ACTION POLICY THAT IS
UTILIZED

2.0 EEO POLICY

1.0 NO REPRESENTATION OR INTENT FOR
REPRESENTATION (EXCLUSIVITY)

At level 1.0, white male dominance in the board room and executive suites is widely evident. These organizations attempt to maintain the status quo by hiring and promoting from within the old boy network.

At level 2.0, organizations at least have an EEO policy that states the intention of the company to broaden its leadership representation to women and minorities. These organizations recognize they need to involve their constituents in the management of the business.

At level 3.0, organizations have and use an affirmative action policy. These organizations actively hire and promote women and members of minority groups for management positions.

At level 4.0, there is aggressive support for internal promotions of women and minorities and evidence of that support on the board and in executive offices. In these organizations differences are not only valued, they are seen as gifts.

At level 5.0, there is meaningful representation of women and minorities among senior management staff and on the board. These organizations see involvement of women and minorities as essential for business success and *in no way* engage merely in token efforts to satisfy public relations goals or government guidelines.

CHAPTER THREE: WINNING WITH CUSTOMERS

Product Development

5.0 ETHICS DRIVE DECISIONS
4.0 ETHICS ARE AN INTEGRAL PART OF DECISIONS
3.0 ETHICS INFLUENCE DECISIONS
2.0 ETHICS ARE CONSIDERED IN DECISIONS
1.0 ETHICS ARE NOT CONSIDERED IN DECISIONS

At level 1.0, products are engineered without thought about the impact on people. In these organizations, the only question is, "What can we sell?"

At level 2.0, ethical questions are entertained in the product "gate review" process, but the emphasis is clearly more technology driven than people driven.

At level 3.0, ethical issues are an important part of the "gate" process. In these organizations, new products or services must pass a basic "ethics test" before they are introduced.

At level 4.0, ethics and decision making are integrally related. In these organizations, if a new product or service does not meet the highest standards of business conduct, it is not introduced.

At level 5.0, product development is driven by ethical issues. In these organizations, the first question is, "What are the major issues our world faces?" And the next question is, "What products or services can we develop to help solve those issues and still achieve our profit objectives?"

Marketing

5.0 INTERDEPENDENT RELATIONSHIPS
4.0 CUSTOMER PRODUCTIVITY
3.0 CUSTOMER BENEFITS
2.0 CUSTOMER SATISFACTION
1.0 CUSTOMER MANIPULATION[18]

At level 1.0, marketing is seen as any way to manipulate the customer to buy a product or service independent of the ethics involved or the benefits provided. Good examples of level one marketing include the home-video purchase approach, in which enthusiastic sales persons hype a variety of products and comsumers can purchase at home by calling a toll-free number. Lotteries would also fall into this category.

At level 2.0, marketing is aimed toward customer satisfaction. Emphasis is a product quality independent of benefit (e.g., much of the food advertising efforts fall into this category).

At level 3.0, marketing is aimed toward real customer benefits. At this level, organizations attempt to fill a niche by demonstrating how the client will benefit from their products or services.

At level 4.0, marketing efforts are designed to show how products or services contribute to improvements in actual customer productivity. The subtle distinction between benefits and added productivity rests in the ability of the producer to understand the customer's frame of reference and his or her particular needs. Level 4.0 organizations encourage their employees to immerse themselves in the customer's business in order to establish better relationships with clients and understand their specific needs. Theoretically, this immersion enables the producer to tailor products and services to given needs.

At level 5.0, marketing efforts revolve around interdependence. At this level, organizations are empowered to openly share information so both organizations may become more productive and profitable. This kind of interdependent marketing requires openness and authenticity. The implication is that the producer will help the consumer make the best possible choice even if that means not choosing the producer's product—the ultimate ethical position. This, of course, raises the question, "Where is the ethical edge in this construct? It sounds like I could only lose." The answer is rhetorical: "With the kind of relationship established through this approach, who else will the consumer turn to?"

CHAPTER FOUR:
WINNING FOR THE COMMUNITY

Environment

5.0 ENVIRONMENTAL LEADERSHIP
4.0 COMMUNITY OUTREACH
3.0 ENVIRONMENTAL PROTECTION
2.0 COMPLIANCE
1.0 STAYING OUT OF TROUBLE

At level 1.0, the company's goal is simply to stay out of trouble. In these organizations, managers will say, "If I don't hear about it and I don't see any obvious disasters, we are doing our job."

At level 2.0, the organization meets the letter of the law. For example, it complies with U.S. environmental legislation such as Sara Title III.

At level 3.0, the company takes a proactive approach to environmental issues. It ensures that all hazardous materials are properly managed, that indoor air quality for its employees is acceptable, and that all waste is properly managed.

At level 4.0, organizations make sure that communities are informed of any toxic chemicals that could be potentially released into the air or water. Efforts are made to curtail air or water pollution, to recycle materials, to conserve energy as best it can, to include environmentally sensitive landscaping and re-vegetation in all building projects, and to avoid billboard advertising.

At level 5.0, the organization takes a leadership role in reducing pollutants, managing waste or reducing chlorofluorcarbons (CFCs).

Resources

5.0   MORE THAN 3% OF PRETAX PROFIT
4.0   3% OF PRETAX PROFIT
3.0   2% OF PRETAX PROFTT
2.0   1% OF PRETAX PROFIT
1.0   LESS THAN 1% OF PRETAX PROFIT

The scale is self explanatory, but it may be helpful to see how many corporations in selected cities meet the level 3 or level 5 goal. The following chart shows the number of corporations in five cities that have joined the 2 percent or 5 percent giving club. Membership in this club means that organizations pledge a certain percentage of their pretax earnings to charity.

	2%	5%
Minneapolis	33	71
Kansas City	107	?
Baltimore	?	53
San Francisco	50	?
Seattle	143	?

Productive Communities

5.0 COMMUNITY INVOLVEMENT REWARDED, PARTICULARLY WHEN IT CONTRIBUTES TO THE CREATION OF PRODUCTIVE COMMUNITIES

4.0 COMMUNITY INVOLVEMENT ENCOURAGED, WITH AN EMPHASIS ON SUSTAINABLE DEVELOPMENT

3.0 COMMUNITY INVOLVEMENT RECOGNIZED/ SUPPORTED

2.0 COMMUNITY INVOLVEMENT ACCEPTED

1.0 COMMUNITY INVOLVEMENT DISCOURAGED

At level 1.0, host communities are only seen as places to set up shop. Employees are discouraged from participating in any community organization. In these organizations, there is disregard for the community consequences of business practices.

At level 2.0, host communities are seen as places where "friendly" relationships are advantageous to business because they may lead, for instance, to favorable zoning decisions. These organizations, therefore, accept employee involvement in community organizations as long as it does not "take away" from time on the job.

At level 3.0, partnership relationships with the host community are encouraged. The community is seen as a resource for talented people, so all parties benefit from effective community development. Thus, employee involvement is recognized and supported.

At level 4.0, the organization's investment and resource decisions are all considered in terms of sustainable development—that is, will the organization's actions have positive, long-term, environmental and economic effects on the community. These organizations encourage constructive community involvement.

At level 5.0, the organization is committed to creating productive communities in which interdependent relationships are established among homes, schools, community organizations and businesses.

APPENDIX B

CORPORATE EXAMPLES

This appendix contains examples of two companies which have tried to define and communicate their codes of conduct and statement of values, respectively. Northern Telecom's code of business conduct is used as the first example and Champion International's statement of values is quoted as the second example.

In most companies, having a code of conduct is a formality. If the code of conduct is not a living part of the culture, it is of limited value.

Northern Telecom is a Canadian based company with 55,000 employees and $6 Billion per year in annual revenues. The company is a leading supplier of telecommunications equipment. Northern Telecom's code of conduct reflects the concerns of a high-tech multinational and is thus directed primarily toward its dealings with outside constituents.

CODE OF BUSINESS CONDUCT: NORTHERN TELECOM

Introduction

Throughout its history, Northern Telecom has maintained high ethical business standards. As the corporation expands into new communities and markets throughout the world, employees, customers, shareholders, suppliers and others should be aware of our ethical standards.

Northern Telecom undertakes to abide by the highest standard of ethical conduct. The corporation supports and encourages its employees to demonstrate the highest ethical standards in their daily business activities. Every Northern Telecom employee is obliged to disclose, through appropriate channels, any act perceived to be a violation of these standards.

However, in a corporation as large and diverse as Northern Telecom, with employees, manufacturing plants and markets around the world, there can be valid differences of opinion about ethical values. Uniform ethics and business practices of multinational companies are not easily established on a global basis. Honesty, integrity, self-discipline, loyalty and compassion are part of almost every society, but the application of these standards often differs from one locality to another.

Northern Telecom operates under a set of broad principles which help employees make ethical decisions in the conduct of corporate business. To further assist its employees, the corporation has formulated policies and guidelines based on these broad principles which illustrate how the principles are to be applied and serve as a guide for employees.

While adhering to these principles and working within the guidelines, employees are also expected to use their own judgement and experience. Northern Telecom expects employees to be honest—with their employer, its customers and other outside parties, and with their fellow workers.

Fundamental Corporate Principles

1. Profit is essential

In our society, profit is the cornerstone of progress and prosperity. Our economic system depends on profit to support the development of our communities, industries, the arts and culture, science, sports, and other social endeavors.

In order to continue in business, commercial enterprises must generate profits to develop new products, build more efficient manufacturing plants, train employees, and invest in other improvements.

Northern Telecom recognizes profits are essential to its continued existence and to the well-being of all those who depend on the corporation. Northern Telecom, therefore, seeks to serve the needs of its customers and employees, while maintaining an appropriate return for its shareholders.

2. Integrity is mandatory in all relationships

A corporation with integrity applies high ethical standards to the conduct of all its affairs. Its ethical principles include honesty, fairness, and respect for individual and community freedoms. It conducts its business at a level well above the minimums required by law.

The same standards apply to a corporation's employees. Employees with integrity do not use their positions in a corporation, or the knowledge they have acquired, to obtain benefits which properly belong to the corporation or the public it serves. All ethical employees avoid conflicts of interest.

Northern Telecom strives to be fair, honest and just in all transactions with customers, shareholders, governments, competitors, suppliers, and others. The corporation willingly accepts and carries out its responsibilities to the community and to the natural environment.

Northern Telecom closely monitors operations to ensure that all employees conduct the corporation's business according to law and its own fundamental corporate principles.

3. A corporation is accountable to its public

All persons with whom a corporation has relationships have a right to know whether it is adhering to stated principles and responsibilities. An ethical corporation is willing to maintain and provide its public with adequate information about its activities. Northern Telecom records all assets, receipts, expenditures, and other transactions in sufficient detail so as to identify their true purpose, source and extent.

Northern Telecom strives to meet all reasonable public requests for information and provides information that is accurate, complete, and understandable, unless the dissemination of such information would weaken the corporation's competitive or proprietary position.

Operating Policies and Guidelines

Northern Telecom has established operating policies and guidelines based on its fundamental corporate principles. These policies and guidelines are intended to indicate to employees what the corporation considers ethical behavior.

The corporation and its employees

The corporation makes every effort to provide job satisfaction, security and occupational opportunity for its employees.

Northern Telecom pays competitive salaries, offers meaningful benefits, strives for stability of employment, provides attractive and safe working conditions, and offers opportunities for personal and professional development to employees.

Corporate policy requires that:

* programs be maintained to protect, conserve and enhance employee health; and

* a safe working environment be provided for all employees.

It is corporate practice:

* to engage people on the basis of their ability to do work assigned consistent with the commitment to be an equal opportunity employer;

* to provide employees with competitive compensation and benefits;

* to safeguard the confidentiality of employee records;

* to promote from within the corporation wherever reasonably possible; and

* to keep employees informed of issues affecting them.

Managing for Achievement is a management process which helps Northern Telecom reach its corporate objectives. This process focuses on defining key job responsibilities for employees, developing objectives, establishing plans, and reviewing individual progress on a regular basis.

Managing for Achievement produces the following benefits:

- a mutual understanding of responsibilities;
- a sound basis for training and development of the individual;
- a climate which fosters achievement and personal growth through communication between managers and their employees.

Conflict of interest

Northern Telecom has established policies to assist employees, officers, and directors of the corporation in avoiding situations which might give rise to conflicts of interest.

It is corporate policy that all Northern Telecom employees, officers, and directors will not:

- appropriate or convert the corporation's property for their own use;
- use or disclose proprietary or confidential information for personal gain or for the gain of others;
- influence in a manner unfavorable to the corporation negotiations or transactions between the corporation and outside suppliers, contrac-

tors, or other organizations in which the employees concerned have a vested interest;

- serve as directors, officers, or employees of, or perform services or consulting work for, any organization which might supply goods or services to the corporation or compete with the corporation, unless the corporation gives its prior approval;

- invest in or control, directly or indirectly, an organization which might supply goods and services to the corporation or compete with the corporation, unless the corporation gives its prior approval;

- accept or offer personal gifts, gratuities or other rewards in order to influence business transactions;

- use their office or position to influence or coerce another employee to do or forgo anything which will result in personal gain; or

- trade in securities of the corporation or any organization with which it has dealings, except in compliance with the relevant securities laws that regulate insider trading, use of non-public information, and trading in securities generally.

The Corporation and Its Shareholders

Shareholders expect a return on their investment commensurate with financial risk.

Northern Telecom endeavors to make investments to ensure acceptable returns while maintaining financial security. In order to maintain shareholders' support, the corporation endeavors to act in what it perceives to be their best interests and informs them promptly of major actions or decisions.

Ethical Practice in the Marketplace

Northern Telecom competes vigorously in a legitimate and ethical manner. This principle is applied to the relationships with customers, competitors, suppliers, and agents and representatives.

Relationships with customers

Customers deserve products of the highest possible quality. Superior product quality includes careful selection of raw materials and components, well-planned and carefully executed production methods, appropriate testing procedures, proper installation by trained personnel, and readily available repair and maintenance service and spare parts.

Product quality also means committing substantial resources to the research, design and development of products and manufacturing technology.

An ethical relationship with customers not only means the provision and service of superior products at reasonable prices, but also the maintenance of ethical standards in those relationships.

Specifically, this means that Northern Telecom employees:

- do not refuse to sell, service or maintain equipment the corporation has produced simply because the customer is buying other products from other suppliers;

- do not make promises the corporation does not intend to keep;

- avoid misrepresentation in all promotional efforts;

- limit customer entertainment to what is reasonable and necessary to facilitate business discussions;

- provide no more than modest gifts to customers in keeping with responsible and generally accepted business practices; and

- do not, directly or indirectly, offer benefits or rewards to customers in violation of laws, regulations or responsible and generally accepted business practices.

Relationships with competitors

Fair competition is the cornerstone of a vibrant economy.

Northern Telecom avoids all actions which could be construed as being anti-competitive, monopolistic, or otherwise contrary to international, national, or local laws governing competitive practices in the marketplace.

Northern Telecom and its employees refuse to associate with or participate in:

- price-fixing schemes;

- bid-rigging arrangements;

- resale price schemes;

- unacceptable exclusive dealings;
- refusals to deal; or
- any similar inappropriate activities.

Northern Telecom and its employees do not disparage competitors and their products, or improperly seek competitors' trade secrets or other confidential information.

Relationships with suppliers

Ethical buying practices involve making decisions on the basis of price, quality, quantity, and service.

Northern Telecom procures materials and services which contribute to the quality of its products and which contribute to the long-term benefit of the corporation.

Employees responsible for buying or leasing materials and services on behalf of the corporation:

- do not accept such gratuities as gifts, money, loans, vacations or other favors from suppliers or potential suppliers, except promotional items of modest value or moderately scaled entertainment within the limits of responsible and generally accepted business practices;
- do not require suppliers to forgo trade with Northern Telecom's competitors; and
- do not require suppliers to buy Northern Telecom products in order to remain a supplier.

Relationships with agents and representatives

Corporations sometimes require the services of an outside person or organization to help market products. In these circumstances, a corporation's relationship with its agents or representatives must be clearly defined and meet high ethical standards.

In some instances, Northern Telecom engages agents or representatives to help the corporation secure or maintain business. Such arrangements are covered by written contracts.

Northern Telecom management is guided by the following:

- compensation of agents and representatives is commensurate with activities undertaken;

- contracts appointing agents or representatives are officially documented in the corporation's records; and

- compensation is recorded in accordance with legal requirements and ethical business practices.

Relationships with the financial community

A responsible, publicly-owned corporation recognizes that its success depends partially on the support of financial analysts, institutional and individual investors, the media, and others in the financial community.

Northern Telecom maintains close, open, and honest relationships with members of the financial community by regularly and willingly informing them about corporate developments.

Northern Telecom Around the World

The obligations of a global corporation to countries where it conducts business extend beyond the payment of taxes and the provision of goods and services.

Northern Telecom policies take into account the social aims and economic priorities of each country in which it does business. The corporation abides by all laws and cooperates with national and local governments, particularly with regard to:

- development of local industry;
- creation of employment, including the promotion of local personnel;
- transfers of technology;
- protection of the environment; and
- maintenance of good employee relations practices.

As a good corporate citizen throughout the world, Northern Telecom does not:

- pay bribes or provide other improper benefits;
- make contributions to political parties or candidates for public office, unless it is customary and legally permissible, and then only within reasonable limits and subject to specific safeguards;
- become involved in covert political activity;
- abuse corporate power to influence public issues;

- withhold or misrepresent financial information for the purpose of evading taxes.

Relationships with Governments

Northern Telecom is committed to the free enterprise system. Such an economic system permits business to function freely within broadly defined limits and allows government to influence the direction of national economies.

Northern Telecom endeavors to conduct its operations without government grants or loans. The corporation believes it is important to avoid or minimize commitments which might restrict the flexibility of its operations.

Northern Telecom does everything it can to be aware of, and comply with, the law in locations where it does business. When appropriate, the corporation offers constructive ideas for changes or improvements to those laws. The corporation does not seek to influence government decisions by unethical means.

Northern Telecom discloses information about all political contributions to the corporation's auditors. The corporation does not reimburse any employee for personal political contributions.

Northern Telecom Is Part of Many Communities

The influence of an enterprise reaches into a multitude of outside communities. These include local communities in which facilities or markets are situated.

Northern Telecom in the local community

A good corporate citizen contributes to the general improvement of the local community.

Northern Telecom directly and through its employees adds to the well-being of the towns, cities and regions where it has manufacturing plants, laboratories, offices, or other facilities.

Northern Telecom contributes to a community's standard of living by:

- cooperating with organizations and individuals to enhance the standing of the community;

- financially supporting worthwhile community programs in such areas as social welfare, health, education, sports, arts and culture, and recreation;

- encouraging employees to participate in local public affairs, charitable organizations, and other community activities of their choice;

- considering the long-term interests of a community when selecting sites for new facilities;

- recruiting local personnel when possible;

- buying materials and services locally when possible; and

- expressing the corporation's views on local and national issues which affect its operations.

The international scientific community

The benefits of technological innovation include a higher standard of living for all people.

While observing national restrictions on transfers of technology, Northern Telecom seeks to share knowledge of product and manufacturing technology as widely as commercial limitations permit. It does this by:

- providing design and manufacturing data to its operations around the world;

- locating research and development facilities wherever they are necessary and economically viable;

- licensing manufacturers in different countries to produce and market Northern Telecom products;

- employing research and development staff from all parts of the world; and,

- encouraging scientific staff and other employees to take part in international associations and conferences, and assisting them to publish the results of their work.

Trade and professional organizations

People working in similar occupations benefit from frequent communication and cooperation with each other.

One of Northern Telecom's principal objectives is to help promote the general welfare of the telecommunications industry and of related professional disciplines.

Northern Telecom supports trade and professional associations both financially and by encouraging employees to join and participate in them.

The corporation works with trade and professional associations to improve international telecommunications standards and to find ways to provide better telecommunications services to society.

Protecting the natural environment

Northern Telecom seeks to make the most effective use of natural resources while striving to protect the natural environment.

The corporation does its part to ensure plentiful natural resources for future generations by:

- using natural resources in a sustainable manner;

- recycling materials whenever feasible;

- designing new facilities to harmonize with their surroundings;

- selecting raw materials and manufacturing processes which have a minimal adverse impact on the environment;

- installing pollution control equipment whenever appropriate; and

- conforming to environmental protection laws and regulations, and subscribing to high standards of environmental protection.

A Statement of Values: Champion International

While the "Champion Way" is a well known statement of ethics, Champion International is not one of the most profitable forest products companies. For 10 years, prior to the end of fiscal year 1988, net return to shareholders was 4 percent. Thus, while we could not include Champion as an exemplar within the body of the book, its statement of values still serves as an excellent example of ethical leadership. We would predict that, at some point in the future, Champion will build its profitability on a sound ethical foundation.

Champion's primary line of business is Forest Products. The Stamford, Connecticut based company has 30,400 employees and generates $5.1 Billion of revenues per year. After a brief period of diversification in the early 1970s, the company returned to its concentration on paper and building products. This consolidation was followed, in 1981, by the formulation and implementation of "the Champion Way"—the corporate culture that the company leaders wanted to establish throughout the organization.

The Champion Way articulates the values that drives the organization. It reads:

> Champion's objective is leadership in American industry. Profitable growth is fundamental to the achievement of that goal and will benefit all to whom we are responsible: shareholders, customers, employees, communities and society at large.

Champion's way of achieving profitable growth requires active participation of all employees in increasing productivity, reducing costs, improving quality and strengthening customer service.

Champion wants to be known for the excellence of its products and service and the integrity of its dealings.

Champion wants to be known as an excellent place to work. This means jobs in facilities that are clean and safe, where the spirit of cooperation and mutual respect prevails, where all feel free to make suggestions, and where all can take pride in working for Champion.

Champion wants to be known for its fair and thoughtful treatment of employees. We are committed to providing equality of opportunity for all people, regardless of race, national origin, sex, age, or religion. We actively seek a talented, diverse, enthusiastic work force. We believe in the individual worth of each employee and seek to foster opportunities for personal development.

Champion wants to be known for its interest in and support of the communities in which employees live and work. We encourage all employees to take an active part in the affairs of their communities, and we will support their volunteer efforts.

Champion wants to be known as a public spirited corporation, mindful of its need to assist—through volunteer efforts and donated funds—non-profit educational, civic, cultural, and social welfare organizations which contribute uniquely to our national life.

Champion wants to be known as an open, truthful company. We are committed to the highest standards of business conduct in our relationships with customers, suppliers, employees, communities, and shareholders. In all our pursuits we are unequivocal in our support of the laws of the land, and acts of questionable legality will not be tolerated.

Champion wants to be known as a company which strives to conserve resources, to reduce waste, and to use and dispose of materials with scrupulous regard for safety and health. We take particular pride in this company's record of compliance with the spirit as well as the letter of all environmental regulations.

Champion believes that only through the individual actions of all employees—guided by a company-wide commitment to excellence—will our long-term economic success and leaderhip position be ensured.

This statement of values not only reflects what's important to Champion's top management, but also indicates how these values are the guideposts for competitive advantage. The fact that seven of the ten statements begin with "we want to be known" demonstrates that Champion believes living by these principles will have many payoffs for the company.

The Champion Way does not stop with an articulate, well-crafted set of statements. Each division is encouraged to "translate" these statements into its own "vision statement." It is understood that these local statements must be consistent with the general statement of the Company, but people have room to personalize the statement to their own particular needs.

Further, executives have communicated that the Champion Way is real through a variety of major decisions that were grounded in the value statements. For example, a recent merger was handled with fairness and most changes were signalled in advance so that employees could take appropriate action. Openness and candor were consistently practiced.

Finally, all employees "participate" in these principles through the *Champion Way in Action* which implores all "Champions" to work together so that "our combined skills, knowledge and experience are utilized as fully as possible." The statement is based on the belief that all employees have more to contribute than traditional management practices have allowed. Thus, the *Champion Way in Action* states, "By changing the way we organize work and the way we manage, we believe that we can gain the needed edge in quality, service and productivity while increasing job satisfaction. The potential—both in profitability and human fulfillment—of more effective individual and group performance—is enormous."

The guiding management practices at Champion emphasize these key values: communications, trust, learning, responsibility, job security, creativity and fairness. Champion takes its value statements seriously. While there are differences in how the Champion Way is perceived at each location and at each level of management, there appears to be a growing consensus that the Champion Way is the "way things really work around here."

REFERENCES

Preface

1. Stoner, C.R. "The Foundations of Business Ethics: Exploring the Relationship Between Organizational Culture, Moral Values and Actions." *Advanced Management Journal*, Summer, 1989.

2. Webster, M., *Ninth New Collegiate Dictionary.* Thomas Allen and Son. Markham, Ontario: 1983.

3. Pastin, M. *The Hard Problems of Management: Gaining the Ethics Edge.* Jossey-Bass, San Francisco: 1986.

4. Stoner, C.R. "The Foundations of Business Ethics: Exploring the Relationship Between Organizational Culture, Moral Values and Actions." *Advanced Management Journal*, Summer, 1989.

5. Feder, B., "Who Will Subscribe to the Valdez Principles?" *The New York Times.* September 10, 1989.

6. Mathews, M. "Corporate Ethical Codes", *Research in Corporate Social Performance and Policy.* Vol 9, ed. by W.E. Frederick. JAI Press, Greenwich, Conn: 1987.

7. Lewis, P, "Ethical Principles for Decision Makers: A Longitudinal Survey," *Journal of Business Ethics,* April, 1989.

8. Frederick, W. and Weber, J. "Personal Value Preference Structures of Corporate Managers and Their Critics. An Empirical Inquiry With Links to Environmental Theory": Paper presented at the Academy of Mangement, August, 1987.

9. Carroll, A. "Managerial Ethics. A Post-Watergate View." *Business Horizons.* April, 1979.

10. Mortensen, R., Smith, J., Cavanagh, G. "The Importance of Ethics to Job Performance: An Empirical Inves-

---

tigation of Managers' Perceptions." *Journal of Business Ethics.* April, 1989.

Introduction

1. Magnet, M., "The Money Society," *Fortune,* July 6, 1987.

2. Shames, L., *The Hunger for More: Searching for Values in an Age of Greed.* Times Books: New York, 1989.

3. Ibid.

4. Lydenberg *et al., Rating America's Corporate Conscience,* Addison-Wesley: Reading, Mass.: 1986.

5. *The 100 Best Companies to Work for in America.*

6. *Rating America's Corporate Conscience.*

7. *The 100 Best Companies to Work for in Canada.*

8. Rockness, J. and Williams, R.A. *A Descriptive Study of Social Responsibility Funds,* July, 1986, working paper, North Carolina State University.

9. Brooks, L. J., *Corporarte Ethical Performance: Trends, Forecasts and Outlooks,* unpublished manuscript, University of Toronto, 1989.

10. Ibid.

11. Brooks, L. J., "Corporate Codes of Ethics." *Journal of Business Ethics,* 1989.

Chapter 1

1. Hay, R. and Gray, E., "Social Responsibilities of Business Managers," *Academy of Management Journal,* March 1977.

2. Sloan, Gruman, Allegrante.

3. Bellingham, R. and Cohen, B. *Managing for Health and Productivity.* Kelly Communications., 1987.

4. Freeman, E.R. and Gilbert, D.R. *Corporate Strategy and the Search for Ethics,* Englewood Cliffs, New Jersey: Prentice Hall, 1988.

5. Bellah, *et al., Habits of the Heart*

6. Peters, T., *Thriving on Chaos.* Knopf, New York: 1987.

Chapter 2

1. Carkhuff, R. R., *The New Age of Capitalism,* HRD Press, Amherst, Mass: 1988.

2. Carkhuff, R. R, *Empowering the Creative Leader.* HRD Press, Amherst, Mass.: 1989.

3. Dertouzos, M., Lester, R., Solow, R., *The MIT Commission on Industrial Productivity,* Made in America, MIT Press, Cambridge, Mass., 1989.

4. Hudson Institute, *Workforce 2000.*

5. Bennett, A. "Company School." *The Wall Street Journal,* May 8, 1989.

6. Ibid.

7. Bellingham, R., Johnson, D., McCauley, M., and Mendes, A., "Projected Cost Savings from AT&T Communications Total Life Concept (TLC) Process," in Chapter 3, *Health Promotion Evaluation,* Edited by Opatz, J., National Wellness Institute, Stevens Point, WI, 1987.

8. Anderson, D., and Jose, W., "Employee Lifestyle and the Bottom Line. Results form the Stay Well Evaluation," *Fitness in Business,* October, 1987.

9. Bly, J., Jones, R. and Richardson, J., "Impact of Worksite Health Promotion on Health Care Costs and

Utilization, Evaluation of Johnson and Johnson's Live for Life Program," *Journal of American Medical Association,* Vol 256, No. 23, December 19, 1986.

10. Health Care Finance Administration, 1988.

11. Ibid.

12. Blue Cross Blue Shield of Maryland, 1989.

13. Centers for Disease Control, Atlanta, 1967.

14. Bird, F.E., *Loss Control Management.* Institute Press, Loganville, Georgia: 1976.

15. Petersen, D. *Analyzing Safety Performance.* Aloray, Deer Park, New York: 1984.

16. Bohlen, D., "Unions Say AT&T Pact Sets New Standards for Family Benefits," *The New York Times,* May 30, 1989.

17. Ibid.

18. Ibid.

19. Gibb-Clark, M., "Firms Meeting Family Needs," *The Globe and Mail,* July 13, 1989.

20. Council on Economic Priorities, *Rating America's Corporate Conscience,* p 23.

21. Ibid.

22. Kesner, I. "Director's Characteristics and Committee Membership. An Investigation of Type, Occupation, Tenure and Gender." *Academy of Management Journal,* Vol 31, 1988.

23. "The Board Game: More Women are Becoming Directors But It's Still a Token Situation", *The Wall Street Journal.* March 24, 1986.

24. *The Economist,* 1987.

25. Fryxell, G., and Lerner, L. "Contrasting Corporate Profiles: Women and Minority Representation in Top Management Positions." *Journal of Business Ethics,* May 1989.

26. "Black Directors in the Corporate Boardroom". *Black Enterprise.* December, 1985.

27. "Black Executives: How They're Doing". *Fortune.* January, 1988.

28. "It Begins with People." *New York Times.* September, 10, 1989.

29. De Pree, M. *Leadership is an Art.* Doubleday. New York, 1989.

Chapter 3.

1. *The Surgeon General's Report. Healthy People.* U.S. Government Printing Office. 1982.

2. Nadel, M., *The Politics of Consumer Protection.* Bobbs-Merrill, New York: 1971.

3. Ackerman, R., *The Social Challenge to Business.* Harvard University Press, Cambridge, Mass.: 1975.

4. Schirmer, W, "Product Liability and Reliability: The View from the President's Office," *Consumerism: Search for the Consumer Interest*, ed. David Aaker and George Day. The Free Press, New York: 1971.

5. Cardin. F., "A Framework for Assessing the Impact of Selected Incentives for Recycling in the Paper Industry." Unpublished thesis. Harvard Business School. Cambridge, Mass.: 1974.

6. Andrews, K., *Ethics in Practice.* Harvard Business School Press. Cambridge, Mass.: 1989.

7. Taylor, F.W., *The Principles of Scientific Management.* W.W. Norton, New York: 1967.

8. Roethlisberger, F. and Dickson, W. *Management and the Worker.* Harvard University Press, Cambridge, Mass.: 1939.

9. Porter, L., Lawler, E. and Hackman, J. *Behavior on Organizations.* McGraw-Hill, New York: 1975.

10. Ackerman, R. *The Social Challenge to Business.* Harvard University Press. Cambridge, Mass.: 1975.

11. Ibid.

12. Ibid.

13. Magnuson, W. and Carper, J. *The Dark Side of Enterprise.* Prentice-Hall, Englewood Cliffs, N.J.: 1972.

14. Peters, T. *Thriving on Chaos.* Knopf, New York: 1987.

15. Ruch, R. and Goodman, R. *Image at the Top.* The Free Press: New York, 1983.

16. Ibid.

17. Carkhuff, R.R. *Winning the Future*, HRD Press. Amherst, Mass.: 1990.

Chapter 4

1. *World Commission on Environment and Development. Our Common Future.* Oxford University Press. New York: 1987.

2–40. Ibid.

41. Carkhuff, R. R. *Toward a Universal Helping Vision.* Keynote Address, International Congress of Psychology, Rome, Italy: 1989.

42. Woolard, E.S., Presentation to the American Chamber of Commerce (UK), London, May 4, 1989.

43. *The Economist,* April, 1988.

44. Interview with David Tostenson, Northern Telecom, July, 1989.

45. Ibid.

46. Council of Economic Priorities. *Rating America's Corporate Conscience.*

47. *Company School*

48. Ibid.

49. Ibid.

50. Ibid.

51. Carkhuff, R.R., *Winning the Future.* HRD Press, Amherst, Mass.: 1990.

Action Steps

1. Carkhuff, R. R., *The New Age of Capitalism.* HRD Press, Amherst, Mass.: 1988

2. Carkhuff, R. R, *Empowering the Creative Leader.* HRD Press, Amherst, Mass.: 1989.

3. Carkhuff, R.R. *Winning the Future.* HRD Press, Amherst, Mass.: 1990.

Summary

1. The World Commission on Environment and Development. *Our Common Future.* Oxford University Press. Oxford: 1987

2. Ibid.

3. Ibid.

4. Ibid.